STUDENT WORKBOOK FOR

Verderber & Verderber's

INTER-ACT

TENTH EDITION

STUDENT WORKBOOK FOR

Verderber & Verderber's

INTER-ACT

**Interpersonal Communication
Concepts, Skills, and Contexts**

TENTH EDITION

Mary Hoeft
University of Wisconsin-Barron County

Sharon Rubin
University of Wisconsin-Barron County

**New York • Oxford
Oxford University Press
2004**

Oxford University Press

Oxford   New York
Auckland   Bangkok   Buenos Aires   Cape Town   Chennai
Dar es Salaam   Delhi   Hong Kong   Istanbul   Karachi   Kolkata
Kuala Lumpur   Madrid   Melbourne   Mexico City   Mumbai
Nairobi   São Paulo   Shanghai   Taipei   Tokyo   Toronto

Published by Oxford University Press, Inc.
198 Madison Avenue, New York, New York, 10016
http://www.oup-usa.org

Oxford is a registered trademark of Oxford University Press

ISBN: 0-19-516910-7

Printing number: 9 8 7 6 5 4 3 2 1

Printed in the United States of America
on acid-free paper

DEDICATION

To Ryan   *From little on, you never hesitated in front of friends*
        to kiss me and say you loved me.
        When Kelly started to attract the attention of your best friends,
        you made it clear they'd better respect her!
        When you emceed the "Miss Aquafest Contest,"
        you were indignant that your little sister didn't win.
        When your friends fell in love, you felt their joy as though it were your own.
        When you fell in love, you shouted it from rooftops.
        Your life wasn't about money or cars or jobs. It was about friends and family.
        For those of us lucky enough to have loved you,
        We will always be touched by your laughter.
        We will always be grateful for your love.

To Kelly   *Your support gives me strength.*
        Your strength gives me courage.
        Your courage gives me the reason to go on.
        Your love reminds me that I'll never be alone.

To Peggy and Larry
        Ryan and Kelly's second parents. My best friends.

To Lois   *No matter how much it hurts, you go outside every night,*
        look up into the stars, find Ryan, and tell him how much he's loved.

To Mom   *You taught me how to love unconditionally.*

To Hannah   *You are the treasure that Ryan left: the twinkle in your eyes,*
        the music in your laughter, keep memories and hope alive.

To my Students at the University of Wisconsin-Barron County
        You remind me daily that work can be fun.

Mary Hoeft

To all those educators who strive to make learning
challenging and meaningful as well as fun and exciting,
especially to two exceptionally talented teachers,
my husband John and my good friend and colleague Mary.

Sharon Rubin

PREFACE

Welcome to the student "manual" that accompanies Verderber and Verderber's *Inter-Act*. Trust me, the word *manual* comes with heavy-duty thought. The editors refer to it as an *ancillary*. Others refer to it as a *workbook*. My son Ryan was the first to term our project a *manual*. I remember being offended. I thought, "This is a lot more than a manual. It's more like a *creation!*"

When I stepped down from my pedestal, I decided that Ryan was right. *Manual* works. Derived from the French word for hands, this manual gives you the opportunity to get your hands dirty as you put Verderber and Verderber's research to the test. So, do it! Roll up your sleeves, and let's get to work as I explain how the manual works.

Interactive Outlines. Each chapter of the manual includes a detailed outline of the corresponding chapter in the text. Brief examples explain how the interpersonal research applies to my life. I ask you to make similar applications.

Key Terms. I have identified a few terms you will want to know if you hope to apply what you have learned in this course. The lists could be much longer, but I had to end somewhere. Here is a challenge: Add terms that you feel should have been included, and share your list with other students.

Activities. I hope you find these activities provocative, useful, and user-friendly. Many give you the opportunity to test the hypotheses of the experts. If a certain project piques your interest, dare to go further. We encourage you to do your own research.

Self Examinations. I hate multiple-choice and true-false exams. There is so much true in every false and so much right in every choice. I subscribe to the Eastern philosophy of Soku: Not one, not two. So, while I have included an answer key at the end of the manual, I might be wrong. I encourage you to argue with my answers. Find true in my false, false in my true, and argue for a better multiple-choice response. A good examination should challenge you to think.

Additional Web Sites. My colleague has identified Internet sites that contain relevant research on topics described within each chapter. I also encourage you to do your own exploration of the Internet.

Sharon and I hope that you find this manual useful. If you have questions or comments, contact us. If you would like to bestow praise, call collect. If you would like to criticize . . . pause a bit . . . review research on constructive criticism . . . and REMEMBER—we're mere mortals.

Mary Hoeft
Department of Communication & Theatre Arts
University of Wisconsin-Barron County
1800 College Drive, Rice Lake WI 54868
mhoeft@uwc.edu

Sharon Rubin
Educational Specialist
University of Wisconsin-Barron County
1800 College Drive, Rice Lake WI 54868

TABLE OF CONTENTS

Chapter 1: An Orientation to Interpersonal Communication

Interactive Chapter Outline

I. Three theoretical concepts are embedded in Verderber and Verderber's definition of interpersonal communication.

    A. Interpersonal communication is transactional. What is happening occurs between the people involved. Meaning is a result of what both participants say and do. You ask your friend out for a sandwich and your friend says, "Not tonight, I'm busy." Discuss the different meanings this exchange could have to your relationship.

        _____

        _____

        _____

    B. Interpersonal communication is a "process." Process means a systematic series of behaviors with a purpose. Think back to what you did today. Identify one conversation that you had with another person and the behaviors that took place.

        _____

        _____

        _____

    C. Through interpersonal communication we create and manage relationships. That meaning may differ for each participant. Suppose Mary's husband says, "What did you do today?" What might Mary read into that question?

        _____

        _____

        _____

    D. Interpersonal communication creates "mutual responsibility" for meanings that are created. If Mary believes that her husband was implying that she did nothing today, what must both do?

        _____

        _____

        _____

II.   Interpersonal Communication affects our social and psychological health.

    A.   Describe a "satisfied" feeling you had following a brief interaction with someone today. What happened that made you feel good?

    _____

    _____

    _____

    _____

    B.   Describe what someone said recently that caused you to see yourself in a positive or negative light.

    _____

    _____

    _____

    _____

    C.   Defy a social convention (i.e. divert eye contact, face back of elevator). Describe the reaction of the other person.

    _____

    _____

    _____

    _____

    D.   Describe a "close" relationship that you have. What takes place in that relationship that causes you to label the relationship close?

    _____

    _____

    _____

    _____

    E.   Have you ever judged someone before you met that person based upon input from a friend? Have you then found out that your judgment was wrong? Explain. _____

    _____

    _____

    _____

    F.   Has someone tried to influence you today? If so, how? Describe your reaction.

    _____

_____

_____

_____

III.   Understanding the elements in the communication process is a crucial step in developing our knowledge of interpersonal communication.

    A.   The message sender (encoder) chooses words, places them in order, and sends the message, hoping that it doesn't get distorted by "noise." Name some "noise" that distorted one of your recent messages.

        _____

        _____

        _____

        _____

    B.   The message receiver (decoder) assigns meaning to (processes) behaviors and words and then offers "feedback." Describe "feedback" you recently sent.

        _____

        _____

        _____

    C.   Research suggests that participants who share similar physical, psychological, and social characteristics have an easier time communicating effectively. Identify the person with whom you communicate most effectively. Then react to the above hypothesis.

        _____

        _____

        _____

        _____

    D.   Context affects expectations, meaning, and behavior.
        1.   Physical context, such as heat, light, and noise, affect the message sent. Describe a physical setting that influenced your behavior.

        _____

        _____

        2.   Social context, such as parent, friend, lover, or enemy, has an impact on communication. Describe your reaction to the following words offered

by a lover: "When I'm near you, my body trembles." Now describe your reaction to the same words offered by your boss.

_____

_____

3. Historical context is the sum of previous communication episodes. For example, Aimee Awonohopay overhears one student say to another, "Hey, give me back that pencil, Indian Giver!" How might U.S. historical treatment of Indians affect her reaction?

_____

_____

_____

4. Psychological context is determined by moods and feelings of each individual. Ryan has just finished his last final. Melissa is cramming for two finals. How might she respond to Ryan's friendly invitation: "Melissa, take a break. You always have your head in a book. Let's take in a movie!"

_____

_____

_____

5. Cultural context is a set of beliefs, values, and norms shared by those communicating. John McCain, presidential candidate and former Navy flier who spent six years in a North Vietnamese POW camp, was described as unapologetic for using the word *gook* to describe his North Vietnamese captors. Following are his words to reporters: "I hated the gooks, I will hate them as long as I live." McCain says he did not use the word to refer to the Vietnamese people, only his captors. Nghi Huynh, publisher and editor of the Asian American Press and a Vietnamese immigrant, said that he believed Vietnamese immigrants would be angered. Explain what happened in the context of beliefs, values, and norms.

_____

_____

_____

IV. Messages are the verbal utterances and nonverbal behaviors to which meaning is attributed.

A. The ideas and feelings that exist in your mind represent meaning. Symbols are words, sounds, and actions that represent ideas. Relate this information to Nghi Huynh's use of the word *gook*.

_____

_____

_____

B. Encoding is the transformation of ideas and feelings into messages. Transforming the message of another is decoding. Describe the feelings that McCain encoded and Nghi Huynh decoded.

_____

_____

_____

V. Noise interferes with meaning. Choose one of the following "noises" and explain how it interfered in a recent conversation.

A. The external noise of sights and sounds
B. The internal noise of thoughts and feelings
C. The semantic noise of unintended meanings

_____

_____

_____

VI. Five basic principles describe interpersonal communication.

A. Interpersonal communication is relational. Linda says to Susan, "Hey, Fat Girl, what's happenin'?" Describe the affect (feeling of affection) and control (domination) in the preceding line.

_____

_____

_____

B. Interpersonal communication is the direct result of learned skills. Paul enters the class, smiles, greets everyone by first name, pulls out a chair for Mia who has just arrived, and waits to take his seat until everyone else has taken theirs. Describe what "Mr. Smooth" learned and where he most likely learned it. Describe some specific interpersonal skills you learned from someone.

_____

_____

_____

_____

C.   Interpersonal communication is purposeful. Sid wants a date with Renee. He sees her in the hall and says, "Renee, how about a café mocha after class?" Renee keeps walking without so much as a pause. Poor Sid was unsuccessful in achieving his purpose. Describe a recent "successful" communication in which you recently engaged.

_____

_____

_____

D.   Interpersonal communication messages may be conscious or unconscious, spontaneous or scripted. Do your messages tend to be more often spontaneous or scripted? Why?

_____

_____

_____

E.   Communication is continuous. Describe a recent message you received that did not involve words.

_____

_____

_____

VII.   Ethical theory tells us what to consider in making decisions.

A.   Personal ethic is based on our personal community or groups with which we identify. What is your personal ethic concerning one of the following: premarital sex, abortion, drinking and driving, and smoking. Relate your personal ethic to the groups with which you identify.

_____

_____

_____

B.   Five key issues form a basis for ethical interpersonal communication:
1.   Truthfulness and honesty are central to ethics and, yet, may pose a moral dilemma. A friend tells you that you are her best friend and **then asks,** "Am I yours?" You like her but do not regard her as your best friend. What would you say?

2.   Integrity involves the ability to resist compromising your morals. If you personally are opposed to abortion and your friend is **going alone** to have an abortion because she has no one else in whom she is willing to confide, do you go with her? Why?

3.   Fairness implies lack of bias. You are president of the PTA. One award will be given to the outstanding student at your elementary school. The names of three finalists have been submitted to you. Your job is to select one. One of the finalists is your child and he/she appears to be the most deserving. What do you do?

4.   Respect is showing regard for another person's rights. Your English professor, while discussing *Canterbury Tales*, refers to Chaucer's use of the word *niggardly*. An African-American student in class is offended. Has the instructor been disrespectful? Why?

5.   Responsibility means accountability for one's actions. An African-American student in the class mentioned above asked the literature teacher to refrain from using the word *niggardly* because the student found the word hurtful. Discuss the instructor's moral responsibility.

VIII. Diversity consideration determines how effectively we communicate.

    A. Culture is a system of shared beliefs, values, symbols, and behaviors. As communicators, we are a product of our culture.

    B. Men and women fail to understand each other because of cultural insensitivity. Explain the dual "insensitivity" that may have existed between the literature professor who used the word *niggardly* and the African-American student.

        _____

        _____

        _____

        _____

    C. Diversity encompasses gender, age, and physical and sexual differences. Discuss the misunderstanding that may occur when a professor says, "During the Salem Witch Trials, angry citizens ignited the **faggots**. Hundreds of women died."

        _____

        _____

        _____

        _____

IX. Competent communicators use appropriate and effective behaviors.

    A. Perceptions of competence depend upon three factors:
        1. Communicator motivation increases competence. If you could care less about making a good impression, it shows.
        2. Communicator knowledge increases competence. Knowing how to behave affects perceptions of competence.
        3. Communicator skill affects communicator competence. Practice of what you know improves the likelihood that you will be able to call upon that wisdom when necessary.

    B. Skills that may improve communication are divided into five categories:
        1. Message-formation skills increase accuracy and clarity of messages we send. Describe an unclear message you recently received.

        _____

        _____

        2. Conversational-climate skills increase the likelihood that we will develop supportive relationships with partners. Are you at ease around someone

in particular? Describe the ease with which you converse with this person.

_____

_____

3.   Listening-for-understanding skills increase the likelihood that we will understand another's meaning. Do you work with someone who never seems to hear what you said?

_____

_____

4.   Empathic-response skills increase the likelihood that we will be able to understand and respond to the emotional experiences of another. Describe the most empathic person you know.

_____

_____

5.   Disclosure skills increase the likelihood that we will share ideas and feelings honestly and sensitively. With whom is it easiest for you to disclose your feelings? Describe a recent situation where you chose not to disclose your feelings. Why?

_____

_____

_____

Of the five skill categories, which do you believe to be your strongest area? Which is the area in which you need the most work?

_____

_____

X.   Setting personal goals will help you to get the most out of the course.

A.   Analyze your current communication skills to determine where you can make improvement.

_____

_____

_____

B.   Write down a description of the change you wish to make. Describe the problem.

_____

_____

_____

_____

C.   Formulate a plan. Describe the specific goal.

_____

_____

_____

D.   Outline a procedure for reaching the goal.

_____

_____

_____

E.   Devise a method for determining when the goal has been reached.

_____

_____

_____

_____

F.   Have another person witness your pledge. Where in your communication are you likely to need the most improvement?

_____

_____

_____

Key Terms in Chapter 1
(Define each of the terms below.)

affect _____

_____

channels _____

_____

communication competence _____

_____

complementary relationship _____

_____

cultural context _____

_____

decoding _____

_____

disclosure _____

_____

diversity _____

_____

empathic _____

_____

encoding _____

_____

ethics _____

_____

external noise _____

_____

feedback _____

_____

historical context _____

_____

internal noise _____

_____

interpersonal communication _____

_____

moral dilemmas _____

_____

physical context _____

_____

psychological context _____

_____

semantic noise _____

_____

social context _____

_____

symbols _____

_____

symmetrical relationship _____

_____

Interesting Sites on the Internet

http://www.towson.edu/~vanfoss/wmcomm.htm#return
> This site reviews research on gender differences in communication, prepared by Dr. Beth Vanfossen, Institute for Teaching and Research on Women, at Towson University.

http://www.bhc.edu/college/ba287/Unit4.htm
> This site contrasts American communication and culture with those of Japan and South Korea as they pertain to the business world.

http://www.bizmove.com/skills/m8g.htm
> This site presents an excerpt from the CD-ROM "Managing A Small Business." The article identifies nonverbal behaviors to which business owners must be sensitive.

http://www.cultsock.ndirect.co.uk/MUHome/cshtml/nvc/nvc5.html
> This site explores the early work of Argyle and Dean in an examination of the relationship between nonverbal communication and perceptions of dominance and affiliation.

http://www.montana.edu/~wwwcommd/effectcomm.html
> David Sharpe, at Montana State University Extension, examines the roles of encoder and decoder in the communication process.

Exercise 1.1

Name _____

She's Easy, Man!

Purpose: To help you recognize that meaning may differ for each participant depending upon context.

Instructions:
A. Pair up with another student in class.
B. Ask your partner what the statements listed below mean.
C. Discuss how close your partner's interpretation of meaning is to your own.
D. Discuss the role that context played in your responses.

_____

1. "He's hot."
2. "She's easy."
3. "He's a jock."
4. "I'm a vegetarian."
5. "She's liberal."

LIST MEANING AND CONTEXT BELOW:

Exercise 1.2

Name _____

Don't Touch Me!

Purpose: To enhance your ability to notice how much others expect you to comply to social norms.

Instructions:
A. Choose one of the following actions listed below.
B. Identify the social norm that you are violating.
C. Perform the "violation" with at least three different people.
D. Identify the reactions of those individuals to your "violation."
E. Discuss with another person in class why you think people responded as they did to the "violation."

_____

1. Divert your eye contact when talking to a friend.
2. Brush your leg against the leg of another student and then don't move it.
3. Touch the hand of another student as you talk to that student.
4. Face the back wall in an elevator.
5. Frown during an entire conversation with a friend.
6. Refrain from making any agreeing sounds or movements when speaking to a friend.

Behavior Chosen: _____

Reactions:

Person #1: _____

Person #2: _____

Person #3: _____

Discussion:

Exercise 1.3

Name _____

Don't Call Me "Girl"!

Purpose: To expand your awareness of words that "trip triggers" in others (semantic noise).

Instructions:
A. Choose one of the following expressions.
B. Use the expression with at least five different people.
C. Identify the verbal and nonverbal reactions of those people.
D. Identify the "semantic" noise that may have caused the reaction that you observed.

_____

1. Address other female students as "girl."
2. Address other male students as "boy."
3. Address adults, with whom you are on a first name basis, as "Mr." or "Mrs.," followed by their last name.
4. Address instructors (could be dangerous) as "Hey you!" or by their first name.

Expression chosen: _____

Verbal and nonverbal reactions:

Person #1: _____

Person #2: _____

Person #3: _____

Person #4: _____

Person #5: _____

Discuss semantic noise:

Exercise 1.4

Name _____

That's Not What I Meant

Purpose: To enhance your ability to understand that meaning may differ for each participant involved in the process of interpersonal communication.

Instructions:

A. Choose a partner.
B. Decide which partner will encode one of the following messages and which partner will decode the message.
C. The "encoder" should write down exactly what you mean prior to sending the message.
D. The "decoder" should tell the "encoder" exactly what you think the message means.
E. The "encoder" and "decoder" should discuss the different meanings.
F. Try to focus your discussion on "context."

---

1. "You're attractive when you smile."
2. "Are you feeling alright?"
3. "Where do you buy your clothes?"
4. "You are such a nerd in class!"
5. "This class rocks!"

Encoder, list below your "intended" meaning:

Exercise 1.5   Name _____

I'd Like to Get to Know You Better!

Purpose: To enhance your awareness of the role that facial expression plays in the decoder's determination of the encoder's "like-ability."

Instructions:

A. Find five pictures of attractive smiling college age people. (Identify each face with a name.)

B. Find five pictures of attractive non-smiling college age people. (Identify each face with a name.)

C. Show the pictures to ten people and ask them to identify, by name, the two people whom they would most like to know better.

D. Tally the responses to determine how many identified people who were smiling and how many identified people who were not smiling.

	CHOICE #1	CHOICE #2
Person #1		
Person #2		
Person #3		
Person #4		
Person #5		
Person #6		
Person #7		
Person #8		
Person #9		
Person #10		

Number of "smiling faces" selected: _____

Number of "non-smiling" faces selected: _____

Exercise 1.6   Name _____

I Promise I'll Be Better

Purpose: To help you to focus your attention on a plan for improving a relationship.

Instructions:
A. Choose one person in your life with whom you would like to communicate better.
B. Place a check in front of the following problems that you believe describe the communication problems in your relationship:
____   1. I don't listen when he/she speaks.
____   2. I don't appear to listen (smile, nod, look of concern) when he/she speaks.
____   3. I interrupt when he/she is speaking.
____   4. I don't initiate a conversation about his/her day.
____   5. I answer questions with only one or two words.
____   6. I don't remember important dates like birthdays.
____   7. I remember important dates but I don't celebrate those dates by planning something special.
C. Make your own personal checklist of interpersonal behavior that you need to work on to improve your relationship with the person mentioned.
D. Choose one item from your personal checklist that you would like to work on and use the form below to devise your plan.
E. Evaluate the success of your plan.

COMMUNICATION PLAN

The communication behavior I would like to improve is:

I will work on improving my communication in the following ways:

Complete these questions following your effort to improve communication:

How successful were my efforts?

What should I try next?

SELF EXAMINATION – CHAPTER 1

True/False   If false, explain what is wrong with the statement.

___ 1. Meaning may differ for each participant.

_____

___ 2. Decoders choose words, place them in order and send them.

_____

___ 3. Too much heat or light affects the social context.

_____

___ 4. Process means one behavior with a purpose.

_____

___ 5. Encoders assign meaning to behaviors and then offer feedback.

_____

Multiple Choice

___ 6. Which of the following definitions best defines "cultural context?"
   A.   beliefs, values, and norms shared by a large group
   B.   moods and feelings of each individual
   C.   sum of previous communication episodes
   D.   factors such as heat, light, and noise

___ 7. Which of the following terms is NOT one of the five major categories highlighted under the topic of context?
   A.   Physical   B.   Social   C.   Historical   D.   Moral

___ 8. Which of the following best describes the five basic principals of interpersonal communication?
   A.   relational, learned, purposeful, unconscious and conscious, continuous
   B.   relational, natural, purposeful, unconscious and conscious, continuous
   C.   relational, learned, purposeful, conscious, continuous
   D.   other-focused, learned, purposeful, unconscious and conscious, continuous

___ 9. Which of the following is NOT a basic principle of interpersonal communication?
   A.   Interpersonal communication is relational.
   B.   Interpersonal communication is purposeful.
   C.   Interpersonal communication results from learned skills.
   D.   Interpersonal communication is always spontaneous.

___10. Which of the following best describes the responsibilities of the encoder?
- A.   chooses words, places them in order, assigns meaning
- B.   choose words, processes behaviors, and offers feedback
- C.   receives message, processes behaviors, and offers feedback
- D.   chooses words, places them in order, sends messages

Complete the Thought

11.   Words, sounds, and actions that represent ideas are referred to as _____.

12.   A systematic series of behaviors with a purpose is _____.

Essay Questions

13.   Explain the five basic principles that describe interpersonal communication.

14.   Explain how external, internal, and semantic noise affect meaning.

Interpersonal Problem Solver

You are the adoptive parent of a child born in Vietnam. You have just been introduced to a man who was a prisoner of war in Vietnam. During your conversation with this individual, he refers to the Vietnamese as *Gooks*. In order to avoid the temptation to immediately label him "racist," how might you apply what you have learned in this chapter about *context*?

Chapter 2:   Forming and Using Social Perceptions

Interactive Chapter Outline

I.   Perception is the process of selectively attending to sensory information and assigning meaning to it.

     A.   The process of perception has three stages:
         1.   We attend to and select stimuli based on our needs, interests, and expectations.
         2.   We organize stimuli.
             a.   We simplify complex perceptions by perusing and labeling what we see. A woman wearing a stethoscope and white jacket is walking down the hallway. We say, "She must be a _____."
             b.   We look for patterns in behavior. Your instructor always smiles when she looks at you.
         3.   We interpret stimuli. What interpretation comes to mind when you see the following? "http" "!!!!" "?" "$"

II.   Social perceptions form the basis of our interpersonal communication.

     A.   Social perception is a set of processes by which people perceive themselves and others.
         1.   Self-concept refers to the idea or mental image you have of yourself based upon your experiences and your understanding of what others think of you. For example, while you may perceive yourself as average looking, your friends see you as drop dead gorgeous. Your self-concept combines both perceptions.
             a.   We can enrich self-concepts of others by "honestly" describing positive traits. Name your most recent effort.   Was it sincere?
             b.   We can damage self-concepts by repeatedly pointing out shortcomings. The crucial word is "repeatedly."   Did someone do that to you? Did you take it to heart? Why?

_____

_____

_____

2.   Self-esteem is your overall evaluation of your competence and personal worthiness.

    a.   High self-esteem depends upon what each individual views as worthwhile. If you are a wonderful cook but don't view cooking as a worthwhile activity, your culinary skills won't enhance your self-esteem. Name one thing you do well and value.

_____

_____

    b.   Self-esteem might become inflated when we focus only on our positive experiences. Identify one "over inflated" ego you know. What is he/she failing to focus on?

_____

_____

_____

    c.   Incongruence is the gap between our inaccurate self-perceptions and reality. If John has an IQ of 160 and perceives himself as stupid, that perception is incongruent. Identify an incongruent perception that one of your friends has of himself/herself.

_____

_____

    d.   Self-fulfilling prophecies are events that happen as a result of being foretold, expected, or talked about. Those prophesies are either self-created or other-created. They reinforce self-concept. People with high self-esteem tend to prophesy success. People with low self-esteem attribute good experiences to luck. Describe one of your most recent "self-fulfilling prophecy" experiences. Do you think it was linked to high or low self-esteem?

_____

_____

_____

_____

3.   Self-perceptions are based upon your personal experiences.

    a.   Self-fulfilling prophecies can distort self-perception. The student who labels himself a "date magnet" based on one or two successful attempts may be anything but a date magnet. Perhaps the women who accepted the dates were desperate or, worse yet, accepted out of pity. Do you know someone whose self-fulfilling prophecies seem to be linked to distortion of self-perception? Explain.

_____

_____

_____

    b.   Filtering can distort our self-perception. If you don't believe that you are beautiful and I tell you that you are beautiful, you may filter my words out. What message do you frequently filter out? Have you learned to accept certain messages that you used to filter out? Name one.

_____

_____

4.   Roles affect identity.
    a.   Working self-concept is the term used to identify specific aspects of one's identity that are activated by the role one is enacting at a particular time. At the moment that you are reading this exercise, what is your "working self-concept?"

_____

_____

_____

    b.   Working self-concepts change as our roles change. Today, Kelly was a daughter, teacher, friend, and lover. What roles have you played today? How have those roles affected your identity?

_____

_____

_____

5.   Self- talk is the process of people "talking" to themselves.
    a.   Self-talk is moderated by self-esteem and self-concept.
    b.   High self-esteem causes us to see others more favorably and influences our self-talk. Dave says, "Lisa, you aren't looking so hot today. Is something wrong?" Lisa feels great. She tells Dave, "I'm feeling fine, Dave, but thanks for asking." For a moment, Lisa self-talks. "I wonder what he saw?" Then she puts it out of her mind, writing it off as Dave just trying to be

thoughtful. Have you had Lisa's experience? Did you have the same reaction that Lisa did? Why?

_____

_____

_____

_____

    c.   Low self-esteem causes us to see others less favorably. If Lisa had low self-esteem she might walk straight to a restroom to see what was "wrong." I've done that. Have you? Explain.

_____

_____

_____

_____

6.   Culture and gender influence perception of self.
    a.   People from the United States tend to value independence. A thirty-five year old man lives at home with his elderly mother. If his self-esteem is derived from the culture in which he lives, this man may view himself as a "momma's boy."
    b.   Eastern cultures and Native American cultures tend to value interdependence. That same man living with his elderly mother may see himself as nurturing.
    c.   In a culture where women are nurturers and men are breadwinners, a working woman may perceive herself has "manly." A stay-at-home father may perceive himself as a "wimp." Identify a perception that you have of yourself based upon your gender.

_____

_____

_____

III.   Perceptions of others result from a process.

    A.   Impressions are formed on the basis of sensory data we take in, organize, and process.

    B.   The uncertainty reduction theory deals with the ways individuals monitor their social environments and come to know themselves and others.

C.   Social perceptions are linked to physical characteristics and behaviors. When you see a woman in black leather on a Harley, what is your perception? When you see a man in uniform on a motorcycle, what is your perception?

_____

_____

_____

1.   Men describe in terms of abilities. "John is a great basketball player." Describe your friend, focusing on three abilities.

_____

_____

_____

_____

2.   Women describe in terms of self-concepts. "She thinks she speaks French well." Describe your friend using a self-concept.

_____

_____

3.   Implicit personality theories are sets of assumptions about physical characteristics and personality traits. "White boys can't jump!" Name another.

_____

4.   Judging by observing a single trait is known as the "halo theory." If Bob opens the door for Mary, I may perceive Bob as a gentleman. Name perceptions that you have made based upon a single observed trait.

_____

_____

_____

D.   Stereotypes are simplified and standardized conceptions about the characteristics or expected behavior of members of an identifiable group

1.   Stereotypes contribute to perceptual inaccuracies. If I enter a hospital and encounter a woman wearing a stethoscope and carrying a chart, I hypothesize that she is a nurse when she is just as likely to be a doctor. Name your most recent perceptual inaccuracy.

_____

_____

_____

2.   Stereotypes provide a "working hypothesis." Pierre is from France. You heard that the French are Socialists. You decide to expound on the values of Socialism only to discover that Pierre is a Capitalist. Tell about the results of your most recent efforts with a working hypothesis.

_____

_____

3.   Prejudice is a negative attitude held toward members of a group. Identify a prejudice of which you have recently become aware.

_____

_____

4.   Racism, sexism, ageism, and able-ism are the beliefs that the characteristics of one group are superior to those of another. Identify one of your "isms."

_____

_____

_____

IV.   Social perception can be improved.

A.   **Watch the behavior of the other person.** You notice that your professor shakes his head when you walk into class late.

B.   **Ask yourself what the behavior means.** You wonder if your instructor is upset that you walked in late.

C.   **Put your interpretation into words.** You ask your instructor, "I noticed you shake your head when I walked into class today. Are you upset that I came late?" Put this 3-step process into practice. Explain a behavior you perceived, ask yourself what it meant, and then put your interpretation into words. Were you correct in your perception? Explain.

_____

_____

_____

_____

Key Terms in Chapter 2
(Define each of the terms below.)

ableism _____

_____

ageism _____

_____

discrimination _____

_____

filter _____

_____

halo effect _____

_____

incongruence _____

_____

interpreting _____

_____

perception _____

_____

prejudice _____

_____

racism _____

_____

role _____

_____

self-concept _____

_____

self-esteem _____

_____

self-talk _____

_____

sexism _____

_____

social perception _____

_____

stereotype _____

_____

uncertainty reduction theory _____

_____

working self-concept _____

_____

Interesting Sites on the Internet

http://mentalhelp.net/psyhelp/chap7/chap71.htm
> Mental Health Net sponsors this site on the roots of prejudice. Material is from Clayton E. Tucker-Ladd's book, *Psychological Self-Help*.

http://www.refresher.com/!blcompliments.html
> Bill Lampton, Ph.D., President of Championship Communication, discusses why paying compliments is as vital as paying salaries.

http://mentalhelp.net/psyhelp/chap14/chap14d.htm
> Mental Health Net sponsors this site on self-concept and self-esteem. Material is from Clayton E. Tucker-Ladd's book, *Psychological Self-Help*.

http://www.serve.com/shea/stereodf.htm
> This site, developed by Robert Shea, educator and Past President of the Missouri chapter of the American Association of Teachers of German, examines the meaning and significance of stereotypes in American culture.

http://www.webster.edu/~woolflm/ageismgender.html
> Linda M. Woolf, Ph.D., Webster University, discusses research that has been conducted concerning ageism of older women and men.

http://www.webster.edu/~woolflm/myth.html
> Linda M. Woolf, Ph.D., provides an Aging Quiz to test your knowledge of common beliefs regarding older adults.

Exercise 2.1

Name _____

You're Looking Down Today

Purpose: To increase your awareness of the fact that perceptions are not always accurate.

Instructions:
A. Observe another student in class in an attempt to determine his/her mood.
B. Using the three-step process of perception, do the following:
  1. Attend to and select stimuli. List what items you focused on.
  2. Organize the stimuli. Look for patterns in behavior. What patterns did you observe?
  3. Interpret the stimuli. What conclusion have you come to concerning his/her mood?
C. Check your perception. For example, "Jim, I noticed that you were paging through the book during class. I also noticed that you had trouble answering when the instructor called on you. Do you need some help with today's assignment?"

List the stimuli that you attended to:

Exercise 2.2

Name _____

You're Drop-Dead Gorgeous

Purpose: To increase your awareness of the role that self-esteem and self-concept play in moderating self-talk.

Instructions:
A. Choose a "flattering" line that suits you. For example, "Hey, you're looking great today!"
B. Choose five people who you really believe are "looking great."
C. Use the line on each of the five people.
D. Record the individual "verbal" and "nonverbal" responses to the line.
E. Discuss why you think they responded as they did.

Reaction of Person #1:

Reaction of Person #2:

Reaction of Person #3:

Reaction of Person #4:

Reaction of Person #5:

Exercise 2.3   Name _____

You're an Angel

Purpose: To increase your awareness of the role that the "halo theory" plays in influencing social perceptions of others.

Instructions:
A. Choose one behavior that others regard as "polite" (i.e. opening a door, pulling out a chair, letting someone step in front of you in a line).
B. Perform this behavior several times throughout the day.
C. Record the reactions, both verbal and nonverbal, of those who benefit from your gesture.
D. Compile a list of your personal behaviors that appear to have a positive influence on social perception.
E. Compile a list of your personal behaviors that appear to have a negative influence on social perception.

List Behavior Used: _____

List Reactions of Others: (both verbal and nonverbal)

List your personal behaviors that appear to have a positive influence on social perception.

List your personal behaviors that appear to have a negative influence on social perception.

Exercise 2.4   Name _____

You Think I Do What???

Purpose: To increase your awareness of the way stereotypes provide us with a working hypothesis.

Instructions:

A. Compile a list of physical characteristics and behaviors that you believe to be typical of any one of the following professions: (working hypothesis)
   1. male college professor
   2. female college student
   3. fraternity member
   4. lawyer
   5. doctor
B. Show your list of physical characteristics and behaviors to a partner and ask the partner to identify the profession of the person you described.
C. Make adjustments to your list of characteristics depending upon what your partner says.
D. Test your working hypothesis to determine whether it proved to be accurate or not.

List characteristics and behaviors of the profession you selected:

Exercise 2.5   Name _____

Wow! Did That Ever Make Me Feel Good!

Purpose: To enhance your overall evaluation of your competence and personal worthiness.

Instructions:
A. Put a check in front of the personal characteristics that you view as most worthwhile. Feel free to add to the list.

1. _____ honesty   6. _____ sense of humor
2. _____ kindness   7. _____ enthusiasm
3. _____ sincerity   8. _____ faithfulness
4. _____ generosity   9. _____ helpfulness
5. _____ compassion   10. _____ patience

B. From the above list, identify the personal characteristic that you view as most worthwhile.
C. Make a list of at least four things that you can do in the following week to work on enhancing the personal characteristic that you identified.
D. At the end of the week, revisit your list and ask yourself the following question:
E. What things did I do that made me feel better about myself (enhanced my self-esteem)?

_____

Personal Characteristic: _____

Four things I plan to do to enhance this personal characteristic:

1.

2.

3.

4.

At the end of the week, ask yourself which activities did the most to enhance your self-esteem.

Exercise 2.6

Name _____

He's So Fragile!

Purpose: To enhance your ability to identify your own personal beliefs that the characteristics of one group are superior to those of another.

Instructions:

A. Ask your partner to give the first name of a person he/she knows who fits the following description:
  1. Nurturing _____
  2. Jock _____
  3. Compassionate _____
  4. Assertive _____
  5. Sensitive _____
  6. Intelligent _____
  7. Talkative _____
  8. Distinguished _____
  9. Flighty _____
  10. Powerful _____

B. Add up how many of the "even-numbered" names on the above list were males and how many were females. (see chart below)
C. Add up how many of the "odd-numbered" names on the above list were males and how many were females. (see chart below)
D. With your partner, discuss your findings. Did the even-numbered list consist mainly of male names? Did the odd-numbered list consist mainly of female names?
E. Discuss the role that sexism, the belief that the characteristics of one group are superior to those of another, played in your partner's choice of names.

Complete the table:	Number
Even-numbered male names	
Even-numbered female names	
Odd-numbered males names	
Odd-numbered female names	

SELF EXAMINATION – CHAPTER 2

True/False   **If false, explain what is wrong with statement.**

___ 1. Judging by observing a single trait is known as the halo theory.

_____

___ 2. Working self-concepts are fixed.

_____

___ 3. Self-esteem refers to the idea or mental image you have of yourself.

_____

___ 4. The process of perception involves attending to, selecting, organizing, and interpreting stimuli.

_____

___ 5. Self-esteem requires that we focus only on our positive experiences.

_____

Multiple Choice

___ 6. Which of the following is NOT true about a stereotype?
   A.   Stereotypes provide a working hypothesis.
   B.   Stereotypes are formed on the basis of sensory data.
   C.   Stereotypes focus on expected behaviors of members of an identifiable group.
   D.   Stereotypes contribute to perceptual inaccuracies.

___ 7. Which of the following does NOT define self-concept?
   A.   the idea you have of yourself
   B.   a mental image of yourself based upon your experiences
   C.   a set of processes by which people perceive others
   D.   an understanding of what others think of you

___ 8. Which of the following statements is NOT true of self-perception?
   A.   Self-fulfilling prophecies clarify self-perception.
   B.   Filtering can distort self-perception.
   C.   Working self-concept refers to aspects of one's identity that are activated by the role one is playing at the moment.
   D.   Working self-concepts change as roles change.

___ 9. The process of perception involves three stages. Which of the following is NOT one of the stages?
A.   attend to and select stimuli
B.   look for patterns
C.   simplify your conception about the expected behaviors
D.   interpret stimuli

___10. Which of the following best defines a stereotype?
A.   an impression formed by judging a single trait
B.   a negative attitude held toward a group
C.   a process by which people perceive themselves
D.   a conception about behaviors and characteristics of a group

Complete the Thought

11.   The term used to identify specific aspects of one's identity that are activated by the role one is enacting at a particular time is _____.

12.   The idea or mental image you have of yourself based upon your experiences and your understanding of what others think of you refers to your _____.

Essay Questions

13.   Social perception can be improved. Explain the three-step process.

14.   Explain the role that self-esteem and self-concept are likely to play in moderating Jeanne's self-talk arising from the following situation: Bob enters Jeanne's apartment. He looks around and says, "Wow, Jeanne, you must be overworked! This place is a mess!"

Interpersonal Problem Solver

You're having a great day! You couldn't feel better. A friend approaches and asks, "Are you okay? You don't look well." Based upon what you know about self-esteem and self-talk, how are you likely to respond and why?

Chapter 3: Communicating in Relationships: Basic Concepts

Interactive Chapter Outline

I. Relationships vary in intensity.

   A. An impersonal relationship is one in which a person relates to the other merely because the other fills a role or satisfies an immediate need.

   B. A personal relationship is one in which people share large amounts of information with each other and meet each other's interpersonal needs.
   1. Friends are people with whom we have negotiated more personal relationships voluntarily.
   2. Some relationships are context bound, i.e. classmates. Do you have relationships that have faded because the context disappeared? Explain.

   _____

   _____

   _____

   _____

   C. We pursue friendships based upon particular qualities or attributes.
   1. Physical appearance is important in the early stages of a relationship and becomes less important as the relationship develops. How important was physical appearance in your last serious relationship? Did the focus on physical importance shift? If so, to what?

   _____

   _____

   _____

   _____

   2. Social skills are important in the early stages of a relationship.
   3. Responsiveness attracts us. Will you continue to pursue an unresponsive attraction? If yes, for how long?

   _____

   4. Similarity of interests, attitudes, values, backgrounds, and personalities

attract us to another. Mutual need fulfillment may draw a quiet person to a talkative person to achieve a "fit." Consider your closest friend. How similar are you?

_____

_____

_____

_____

D.   Healthy relationships involve balanced behaviors.

    1.   They are marked by balanced self-disclosure (sharing biographical data, personal ideas, and feelings that are unknown to the other person). How do you feel when a friend fails to self-disclose? Why?

_____

_____

_____

_____

    2.   They are marked by balanced feedback (the verbal and physical responses to people and/or their messages).

E.   The Johari window is a tool for examining the relationship between disclosure and feedback.

    1.   **Quadrant 1, the open pane**, represents information about you that both you and your partner know. Mary tells Louise that she ended her relationship with Dave because they didn't have enough in common.

    2.   **Quadrant 2, the secret pane**, contains information that you know about yourself but your partner does not know. Mary is HIV positive. Louise doesn't know.

    3.   **Quadrant 3, the blind pane**, contains information that your partner knows about you but about which you are unaware. For example, Mary has bad breath but doesn't know it. Her friend Louise does. Louise also thinks that Mary has an abrasive personality but has never mentioned it to Mary.

    4.   **Quadrant 4, the unknown pane**, contains information that neither you nor your partner knows. Until you both try something, neither of you knows how the experience will unfold. Mary has always wanted to move to New York. She thinks she will love it. Neither she nor Louise know how Mary will respond if she moves.

Think about your "best" friend. Design a Johari window that describes your relationship.

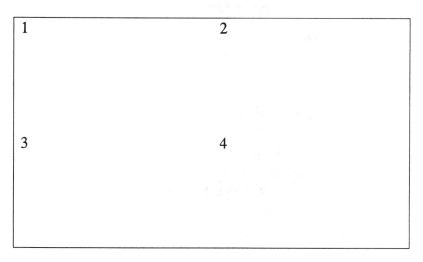

II.   Relationships exist because they satisfy basic human needs.

A.   Schutz's Interpersonal Needs Theory proposes that whether or not a relationship is started, built, or maintained depends on how well each person meets the interpersonal needs of the other.

B.   The need for affection varies in individuals. Which of the following individuals best describes you? Explain.
1.   Underpersonal individuals avoid close ties and seldom show strong feeling toward others.
2.   Overpersonal individuals thrive on establishing close relationships with everyone.
3.   Personal people express and receive affection.

_____

_____

_____

_____

_____

_____

C.   The need for inclusion reflects a desire to be in the company of other people. Which of the following individuals best describes you? Explain.
1.   Undersocial people usually want to be left alone.
2.   Oversocial people need constant companionship.

_____

_____

_____

_____

_____

D.   The need for control reflects a desire to influence the events and people around us. Which of the following individuals best describes you? Why?

    1.   Abdicrats are extremely submissive, unlikely to make decisions or accept responsibility.

    2.   Autocrats need to dominate.

    3.   Democrats need to lead at certain times and follow at others.

_____

_____

_____

_____

_____

III.   Relationships can be analyzed on the basis of exchange ratios.

A.   Thibaut and Kelley's Exchange Theory says that relationships can be understood in terms of the exchange of rewards and costs that take place during the individuals' interaction.

    1.   Rewards are outcomes that are valued by a person. Rewards include good feelings, prestige, and economic gain. What rewards do you value in your current relationships?

_____

_____

_____

_____

_____

    2.   Costs are outcomes that a person does not wish to incur. Costs include time, energy, and anxiety. What costs are you least willing to incur in your current relationships?

_____

_____

_____

_____

_____

B.   People seek high reward and low cost interactions.
1.   The desirable ratio between cost and reward varies from person to person. Try to analyze costs and rewards in your current relationships.

_____

_____

_____

_____

2.   People with a number of good cost/reward relationships will probably not be satisfied with low-outcome relationships. Are you quick to abandon low-outcome relationships? Think about the last relationship you abandoned. Why did you abandon it?

_____

_____

_____

_____

_____

3.   People with few positive interactions will be satisfied with relationships that people with high-outcome relationships would find unattractive.
4.   People sometimes continue an "unfulfilling" relationship because it is no worse than most of their relationships. Have you ever maintained a relationship because you didn't think anything better was available? What happened to the relationship?

_____

_____

_____

_____

_____

IV.   Communication is crucial to a lasting relationship.

A.   We need to gather much information about the person to whom we are attracted (uncertainty reduction). Which of the following strategies do you tend to employ most often? Why?
1.   Passive strategy involves observation.
2.   Active strategy involves asking others.

3.   Interactive strategy involves conversing with the person in question.

_____

_____

_____

_____

B.   Duck's Theory says how we talk is crucial to building a relationship.
1.   How we talk with another may be the most important variable in starting and building relationships.
2.   What happens in the first few minutes of an initial conversation will have a profound effect on the nature of the relationship.

C.   Four strategies assist in starting conversations with strangers. Do you use these strategies? Why?
1.   Introduce yourself and ask other person's name.
2.   Refer to the physical context and ask the other person's opinion.
3.   Refer to your thoughts or feelings and ask the other person's opinion.
4.   Refer to the other person and ask a question.

Pair up with another person in class and try to get to know that person using the four strategies listed. Remember to use a question at the end of each strategy to draw the other person into the conversation. Write out your planned conversation:

_____

_____

_____

_____

D.   Small talk, conversation that meets social needs with relatively low amounts of risk, helps to keep a conversation going.
1.   Idea exchange communication involves sharing of facts, opinions, and beliefs.
2.   Gossip is the relating of information whose accuracy may be unknown. At times unethical and malicious, it is one of the most common forms of interpersonal communication.

How effective are you at small talk? How do you rate yourself as a gossip?
Are you pleased with that rating? Why?

_____

E. Intimate levels of conversation involve serious ideas and affectionate communication.
   1. Affectionate behaviors include holding hands, sitting close, looking into eyes.
   2. Affectionate words involve relationship statements like "I value our friendship."
   3. Feelings and highly personal information are disclosed. React to Verderber and Verderber's account of a relationship between a paraplegic and an able-bodied person. If their relationship is moving toward intimacy, what conversation is he likely to have with his partner?

F. Once relationships have been established, a positive climate for communication must be fostered through the use of four related skills. Consider a close friendship that you have. How effectively do you use the following skills?
   1. **Speak descriptively**.
      a. Focus on descriptions of behavior and descriptions of feelings. "Sue, when you rolled your eyes at me in front of my friends, I felt embarrassed and hurt."

      b. Avoid evaluative responses that may result in defensiveness. "Sue, you jerk, stop rolling your eyes at me!" Sue responds, "Well, I'll stop rolling my eyes when you stop talking like such an idiot!"

   2. **Speak openly.**
      a. Share true thoughts and feelings.

      b. Avoid hidden agendas, secret underlying motives for holding a conversation.

3.   **Speak provisionally.**
       a.   You think the ideas are correct but they might not be.
       b.   Avoid dogmatic statements that leave no room for discussion.
       Restate the following phrase provisionally: "I'm certain I told you that the movie started at 9:00. You don't listen!"

_____

_____

_____

4.   **Speak to others as equals.**
       a.   Exclude words of superiority.
       b.   Exclude nonverbal signs of authority.
       Restate the following line as an "equal": "I'm your mother, for heavens sake. Show me some respect!"

_____

_____

_____

_____

V.   Signs indicate a weakening relationship. Consider a relationship of yours that appears to be weakening. Are the following signs evident? If so, explain.

   A.   Subtle indications of dissatisfaction appear. Touchy subjects surface. Explain.

_____

   B.   People drift from deep sharing of ideas to small talk. Explain.

_____

VI.   Strategies mark the end of a relationship. Consider a relationship of yours that ended. Which, if any, of the following strategies were used? Explain.

   A.   Manipulative strategies involve intentionally presenting evidence of a serious breach of faith and leaving the other party to take action.

   B.   Withdrawal/avoidance strategies use indirect methods to achieve termination.

   C.   Positive tone strategies involve open, honest communication.

_____

_____

_____

_____

_____

Key Terms in Chapter 3

(Define each of the terms below.)

affection _____

_____

control _____

_____

defensiveness _____

_____

exchange theory _____

_____

feedback _____

_____

hidden agenda _____

_____

impersonal relationship _____

_____

inclusion _____

_____

interpersonal needs theory _____

_____

Johari window _____

_____

provisional speaking _____

_____

self-disclosure _____

_____

small talk _____

_____

stabilization _____

_____

uncertainty reduction _____

_____

withdrawal _____

_____

Interesting Sites on the Internet

http://www.findarticles.com/cf_dls/m1175/3_34/73537491/print.jhtml

    Nigel Nicholson, Professor of Organizational Behavior at London Business School, relates the role of gossip in this article taken from *Psychology Today*.

http://www.dallas.net/~scotpeck/saleswebpage/conver.htm

    Scott Peck Marketing and Sales Consulting presents a list of "conversation openers" that encourage the listener to share thoughts and feelings.

http://www.susanroane.com/books_tapes/booksaynextchap1.html

    This site presents Chapter 1 from Susan RoAne's book *What Do I Say Next?* The author explores how to develop and enhance conversational prowess.

http://www.drnadig.com/conflict.htm

    Larry Nadig, clinical psychologist and marriage and family therapist, examines the healthy side of conflict in relationships and offers approaches to healthy conflict resolution.

http://www.loveadvice.com/ARTICLES/ENDINGIT.HTM

    Dr. Tracy, author of the book *Letting Go*, offers advice on how to end a relationship with class and style.

Exercise 3.1   Name _____

I'm the Boss

Purpose: To increase your awareness of the impact that your words have on others.

Instructions:
A. Role play the following scenario: You have developed the reputation of being a know-it-all. You don't like the reputation and are determined to work on it.
B. Below is one of your typical conversations with your friend.
C. With a partner, find ways to adjust the following lines to show that you are an "equal" and not a "superior" in this relationship.

Lines:
1. "Let's party tonight."
2. "Let's go to the bar. There's a live band."
3. "After the bar, we can go to TGI Friday for a sandwich."
4. "You drive."
5. "Don't be late!"

Revised "equal" lines:

Exercise 3.2   Name _____

It's Over! Kaput! Fini! Ciao, Baby!

Purpose: To enhance your ability to use "positive tone" strategies to end a relationship.

Instructions:

A. Read the following scenario: You have been dating another person for six months. Your partner is happy with the progress of the relationship. You are not. You have decided to end the relationship. In ten sentences, explain, as clearly and affirmingly as possible, the reason that you are about to terminate the relationship.

B. Pair up with another person of the opposite sex. Read your ten sentences to this person. Decide if the ten sentences are indeed positive. Try to determine if the ten sentences included some manipulative strategies or withdrawal/avoidance strategies.

Write your ten sentences below:

Exercise 3.3

Name _____

You Don't Begin to Know Me

Purpose: To help you to better understand the Johari window, a tool that will enhance your ability to examine the relationship between disclosure and feedback.

Instructions:

A. Study the two Johari windows below. Sandy and Wayne are university students who have been dating exclusively for six months. Sandy and Wayne have completed Johari windows describing their relationship in terms of intimacy and truth.

B. Describe the relationship from Sandy's perspective.

C. Describe the relationship from Wayne's perspective.

WAYNE

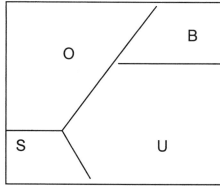

SANDY

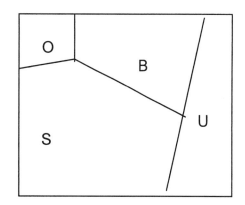

Describe Wayne's perception of the relationship:

Describe Sandy's perception of the relationship:

Exercise 3.4   Name _____

What's Wrong with You? Is Your Tongue Tied?

Purpose: To learn how to use more effective "small talk."

Instructions:
A. Prepare three lines of conversation using the following steps:
   1. Casually introduce yourself and ask stranger's name.
   2. Make a reference to the physical context (weather, trees, room, temperature, view, etc.).
   3. Make a reference to your thoughts/feelings about something and ask for the stranger's thoughts.
B. Use the lines that you prepared in the following situations:
   1. Seek out a stranger in the Student Union.
   2. Seek out a stranger in the library.
   3. Seek out a stranger on the way to class.

_____

Record the reactions of each participant to the "small talk" exercise:

Stranger #1: _____

Stranger #2: _____

Stranger #3: _____

Discuss your reactions to how effective your attempts at "small talk" were:

Exercise 3.5   Name _____

You'll Always Be My Friend! At Least Until Tomorrow!

Purpose: To increase your awareness of fulfilled and unfulfilled personal needs in your present friendships.

Instructions:
A. Identify the name of one of your college friends.
B. Using the following check list, identify with an *x* the qualities or attributes you find most appealing in this friend.
C. Using the same check list, identify with an *o* the qualities or attributes you find least appealing in this friend.

Name of friend: _____

Place an *x* in front of the qualities or attributes you find most appealing in this friend.
Place an *o* in front of the qualities or attributes you find least appealing in this friend.

FRIENDSHIP CHECK LIST

_____ attitude about school	_____ good looking
_____ attitude about work	_____ well-dressed
_____ attitude about life	_____ compassionate
_____ attitude about money	_____ well-mannered
_____ attitude about friendships	_____ ambitious
_____ willingness to share feelings	_____ thoughtful
_____ willingness to listen	_____ generous
_____ willingness to accommodate my needs	_____ fun-loving

Based upon the items you have marked, what chance do you give this friendship of surviving? Why?

Exercise 3.6

Name _____

I Can't Afford This Friendship

Purpose: To increase your awareness of the costs that some friendships incur; costs that outweigh the rewards.

Instructions:

A. Identify the name of one person who used to be your friend but no longer is.
B. List the rewards, outcomes that you personally valued, in that friendship.
C. List the costs, outcomes that you did not wish to incur, in that friendship.
D. Examine the list of rewards and costs in order to determine whether the friendship ended due to the low reward/high cost ratio.

Name of "lost" friend: _____

List of **rewards** incurred in the friendship: (i.e. good feelings, prestige, economic gain)
1.

2.

3.

4.

5.

List of **costs** incurred in the friendship: (i.e. time, energy, anxiety)
1.

2.

3.

4.

5.

After examining the above lists, what role, if any, do you believe "high costs" played in ending the friendship?

SELF EXAMINATION – CHAPTER 3

True/False   If false, explain what is wrong with the statement.

____ 1. Quadrant 4 of the Johari window contains information that neither you nor your partner knows.

_____

____ 2. Duck's theory of communication says small talk is crucial to building a relationship.

_____

____ 3. A personal relationship is one in which a person relates to the other merely because the other fills a role.

_____

____ 4. Physical appearance becomes more important as the relationship develops.

_____

____ 5. Passive strategy of communication involves asking others.

_____

Multiple Choice

____ 6. Which of the following statements best illustrates provisional speech?
   A.   "Darnell, I gave you the letter yesterday."
   B.   "Jordan, you weren't in class yesterday, were you?"
   C.   "Sherwana, I'm certain you told me that story last week."
   D.   "Brogan, when you rolled your eyes at me, I felt embarrassed."

____ 7. The Johari window is a tool for examining the relationship between disclosure and feedback. Which of the following is NOT a pane in the window?
   A.   open pane representing information about you that both you and your partner know
   B.   blind pane containing information that your partner knows about you but you don't
   C.   dark pane containing information that both you and your partner know and refuse to share
   D.   unknown pane containing information that neither you nor your partner knows

____ 8. Schutz's Interpersonal Needs Theory proposes that relationships are based upon needs. Which of the following is NOT one of the needs mentioned in Schutz's theory?
   A.   submission   C.   inclusion
   B.   control   D.   affection

___ 9. In examining the relationship that you have with your partner, which quadrant of the Johari window represents information that is known to both you and your partner?
- A. quadrant 1
- B. quadrant 2
- C. quadrant 3
- D. quadrant 4

___ 10. The need for control varies in individuals. Which answer best describes an Abdicrat?
- A. dominates
- B. submits
- C. leads and follows
- D. accepts responsibility for decisions

Complete the Thought

11. "I'm not certain, Aaron, but I think you already saw that movie" is an example of speaking referred to as _____.

12. "You Jerk!" is an example of speaking referred to as _____.

Essay Questions

13. Describe the four strategies that assist in starting conversations with strangers.

14. Once a close relationship has been established, discuss the four skills that will assist in fostering a positive climate for communication.

Interpersonal Problem Solver

You have had two dates with someone. You feel totally at ease and have no trouble making small talk. You are about to go on a third date. You realize that you are starting to have strong feelings for this person. Without coming right out and saying so, what can you do and say to convey that you have moved to a greater level of intimacy?

Chapter 4: Verbal Communication

Interactive Chapter Outline

I.   Everyone lives in a speech community.

    A.   A speech community is a group of people who speak the same language.

    B.   There are between 3,000 and 4,000 speech communities in the world.

    C.   60% of those communities have fewer than 10,000 speakers.

    D.   The largest speech communities, in order, are:
        1.   Mandarin Chinese
        2.   English
        3.   Spanish
        4.   Arabic
        5.   Hindi

II.   Through language we communicate within our speech community.

    A.   **We use language to name, describe, classify, and limit.** For example, "Sharon is my good friend, and the co-author of this interpersonal communication manual." Name, describe, classify, and limit one of your acquaintances.

    _____

    _____

    B.   **We use language to evaluate.**
        1.   **Words can have a positive slant.** I might describe my slender friend by saying, "She has a model's figure." "She's petite."
        2.   **Words can have a negative slant.** I might describe the same friend by saying, "She's as skinny as a rail." "She's a toothpick."
My daughter cleans off her dinner plate with her index finger. Some describe her gesture as gross. She describes the behavior as a "logical" way to scoop up leftovers. Put both a positive and negative slant on your language as you describe a friend who does the following: "moons you in a public place," "passes gas in class," "belches at the dinner table," "offers you the finger."

    _____

    _____

    _____

_____

_____

C. **We use language to discuss things outside our immediate experience, whether in the past, present, or future.**
1. We speak hypothetically with language. For example: "If I were rich..."
2. We talk about the past and future. "When my son was a child..." "One day, when my daughter has children..."
3. We communicate about people and things not present.

D. We use language to talk about language. One student might refer to a professor's lecture as "boring," another might call it "confusing," and still another "inspiring."

III. The relationship between language and meaning is complicated.

A. We are not born knowing language. Each generation learns it anew.

B. Younger generations invent new words and new meanings for words. For example: What is a cheese box?

C. Each utterance is a creative act. My son, when he was two, used to call my crystal-filled living room the *No No* room. What words have you and your friends created?

_____

D. People interpret words differently.
1. **Denotations**, the explicit meanings found in the dictionary, are multiple and change over time. Use a new dictionary to search for the varied denotative meanings of the word *cool*.

_____

2. **Syntactic context**, the position of a word in a sentence and the other words around it, affects meaning. If I said, "On a hot day last week, I saw my friend's hot roommate walking across campus," how does the denotative meaning of *hot* vary depending upon its syntactical context?

_____

_____

3. **Connotation**, the feelings or evaluations we personally associate with a word, are important to understanding meaning. The subjective reaction

of a person is determined by his/her life experiences. Discuss with a partner, the connotative meaning you personally associate with the following words: *AIDS, cancer, euthanasia, adultery, masturbation, homosexuality, war.*

_____

_____

_____

_____

_____

_____

IV.   Meanings vary across speech communities and among subgroups in a single speech community.

   A.   Dialects are variations on a core language that allow a subgroup in a speech community to share unique meanings.
      1.   The official dialect of a speech community is the privileged form taught in school.
      2.   The official dialect of a speech community becomes the standard by which other dialects are judged. My colleague from Arkansas was lovingly teased by her Northern Wisconsin students about the funny way she spoke. What dialects stood out in your speech community as *funny*?

   _____

   _____

   In the U.S. job market, standard English marks an educated person. How well is a job candidate likely to fare if, during an interview, he/she says, "I ain't afraid of hard work"?

   B.   Cultural differences exist within speech communities.
      1.   Cultures differ in how goals are emphasized and communicated.
         a.   **Individualistic cultures emphasize individual goals more than group goals.** Speakers communicate using low-context communication where information is presented directly.
         b.   **Collectivistic cultures emphasize group goals more than individual goals.** Speakers use high-context communication where others are expected to know what the speaker is thinking and feeling, and the message is presented indirectly.

How might a **collectivistic, high-context communicator** respond to the following job interview question? "Ten years from now, what do you envision your role to be with our company?"

_____

_____

_____

How might an **individualistic, low-context communicator** respond to the same question?

_____

_____

_____

Describe the problems that a collectivistic, high-context communicator and an individualistic, low-context communicator might incur if they were to marry.

_____

_____

_____

_____

2.   Cultures differ in how comfortable they are with uncertainty.
    a.   **Low uncertainty avoidance** cultures are **more comfortable with uncertainty.**
    b.   **High uncertainty avoidance** cultures are **uncomfortable with uncertainty.**
    If you were invited to go backpacking through Europe with no particular destination or timeline, how comfortable would you be with the uncertainty? Why?

_____

_____

_____

3.   Cultures differ in adherence to traditional sex roles.
    a.   Masculine cultures are those in which people are expected to maintain traditional sex roles.
    b.   Feminine cultures are those in which men and women are expected to take a variety of roles.
4.   Cultures differ in their view and treatment of powerful people.
    a.   High power-distance cultures show respect for the powerful.
    b.   Low power-distance cultures play down power inequalities, resulting in less deferential language.

Based upon your understanding of cultural differences, where would you place yourself? Individualistic or collectivistic? Low or high uncertainty avoidance? Masculine or feminine? Now identify a friend or acquaintance, born in the U.S., whose culture is different from your own. In which categories would you place him/her? What communication difficulties, if any, have you experienced?

_____

_____

_____

_____

_____

_____

C. American listeners prejudge based upon accents (Diverse Voices).
1. Speakers with a standard American accent prejudge speakers with other accents to be less intelligent and less status-possessing. My colleague from Arkansas felt as though she was being "talked down to" by her Northern colleagues because of her accent.
2. Speakers with nonstandard accents often prejudge similar nonstandard accent speakers to have low standing.
3. Standard American accented speakers are selective as to how they perceive foreign accented speakers.
   a. British-accented speakers are perceived as equal.
   b. Foreign-born university professors are frequently judged inadequate based upon accent.

When my son was a college freshman, he called to say he couldn't understand what his foreign-born math professor was saying. I advised Ryan to stay in the class long enough to determine whether the problem was Ryan's lack of comfort with the speaker's accent or whether it was a more serious problem. As it turned out, the TA's grasp of English was so weak that he lacked the vocabulary to explain complex concepts in a way that students could understand.

Have you ever dropped a class taught by a foreign-born professor? Was there additional information beyond his/her accent that caused you to drop the class? Have you remained in a course taught by a foreign-born professor? What role did factors, other than accent, have on your perception of the professor?

Some differences in language usage between men and women exist.

A. Women tend to use more intensifiers and hedges.

1. Intensifiers modify words and strengthen the idea. For example: "She is a very intelligent woman." "He's really nice." List modifiers that you repeatedly use.

   _____

2. Hedges are modifying words that soften or weaken meaning. For example: "I think that I understood his point." Name more.

   _____

B. Women ask questions more frequently.

C. Female speakers are rated as having higher social status, being more literate, and being more pleasant.

D. Male speech is perceived as stronger and more aggressive.

In the next week, observe two of your professors, one male and one female, listening specifically for answers to the following questions: Who used more intensifiers? Hedges? Asked more questions? Appeared more pleasant? Discuss your results with a partner.

VI. Language clarity can be increased.

A. **Increase your vocabulary.**
   1. Study vocabulary like the "Word Power" feature in *The Reader's Digest*. Name additional sites.

      _____

   2. Find definitions to new words you encounter. In the next week, make a list of ten words that you hear speakers use. Find the definitions. I'm sure you've heard the following words before. With a partner, define them: *innocuous, eristic, lugubrious, salacious.*

      _____

      _____

      _____

      _____

B. **Choose specific language.**
   1. Specific words clear up ambiguity.
   2. Specific words are more concrete than general words. A general word that describes my car is *old*. More specific than old is *twelve years old*.

3.   Specific words are precise. Rather than saying you plan to purchase an economy car, you might say, "I'm buying a Neon."

4.   Specific words provide details and examples. Can you provide an example that would make one of the following statements more specific? "My blind date was a disaster." "My parents are strict." "My friend is an oddball."

_____

_____

C.   **Acquire and use accurate information.** For example: If I were speaking to a friend about life expectancy and said, "Native Americans have a lower life expectancy than people of other races," I would strengthen that statement if I could back it up with research: "According to Tex Hall, president of the national Congress of American Indians, Indians have a life expectancy that is five years shorter than any other race."

D.   **Date information by specifying the time or time period that the fact was true or known to be true.** For example: "On February 1, 2003, Tex Hall, president of the National Congress of American Indians, in his first State of the Indian Nations address, said . . ."

E.   **Index generalizations by acknowledging the presence of individual differences.**

1.   Misuse of generalizations contributes to perceptual inaccuracies.

2.   Misuse of generalizations ignores individual differences.

Unindexed generalization: Because the terrorists in the September 11 attack on the Twin Towers have been linked to Al-Qaeda, we can be certain that Osama Bin Laden masterminded the attack.

Indexed Generalization: Because of the link between the September 11 terrorists and Al-Qaeda, it is likely that Osama Bin Laden played a role in the attack on the Twin Towers, although others may have been involved.

Develop an indexed generalization in response to the following question: Who shot John Fitzgerald Kennedy?

_____

_____

_____

_____

VII.   Strategies exist for crafting appropriate verbal messages.

A.   Language should be appropriately geared to the formality of the situation.
How would you appropriately greet the following:

Your Chancellor: _____

Your favorite professor: _____

A State Representative: _____

The Prime Minister of England: _____

A State Supreme Court Justice: _____

Your parents: _____

When my daughter was in sixth grade, her new friend Erin came to our house. She greeted me with, "Hello, Mrs. Hoeft." I responded with, "Call me Mary." She said, "Oh no, my father told me that it was disrespectful to call parents by their first name." What is your reaction to Erin's response? Why?

_____

_____

_____

_____

B.   Avoid or define jargon and slang.

1.   Jargon is technical terminology whose meaning is idiosyncratic to a special activity or interest group.
Do you know what the following computer-friendly students are talking about? If so, explain: "I can't believe how much spam I got today." "Did you catch that worm that's been going around?" "I turned my cookies off."

_____

_____

_____

2.   Slang is informal, nonstandard use of vocabulary. In the 1960s, a good looking woman was a "hot chick." Today, what is she? In the 1960s, my apartment was my "pad." What is it today? In the 1960s, the popular kids were "hip" and "cool." What are they today? Create a list of the slang in your everyday vocabulary. Share that list with your professor and see if he/she knows what the words mean. (I had no idea what two of my students were talking about yesterday when I overheard one ask if the other had made a "booty call.")

_____

_____

_____

_____

C. Avoid crude language.
    1. Use of vulgarity and profanity asserts a form of independence by breaking taboos.
    2. Verderber and Verderber argue that speakers who use vulgarities risk being perceived as crude, uneducated, and menacing. Does your language with friends include profanity or vulgarity? If *yes*, do you believe that the use of profanity has a negative impact on your relationships? Explain. If swearing is a part of your language, are there people around whom you are careful not to swear? Who? Why?

_____

_____

_____

_____

_____

_____

D. Demonstrate sensitivity.
    1. **Avoid generic language that applies only to one sex, race, or other group as though they represent everyone.**
        a. Use plurals. Instead of "each student should hand in his assignment on Tuesday," what might you say?

_____

        b. Use both male and female pronouns. "If a student were to hand in his or her assignment late . . ."
        c. Avoid words that include generic use of the word *man* to ensure that listeners visualize both men and women.

Write a generic equivalent that ensures that listeners visualize both men and women:

"Please man the phone while I have lunch."_____

"All men are created equal."_____

"A man's home is his castle." _____

"I am my brother's keeper." _____

"I'm a lineman for the county." _____

"It's a man-eating shark." _____

Write a generic equivalent to the following terms to ensure that listeners visualize both men and women:

postman _____ *policeman* _____

meter maid _____ *stewardess* _____

fisherman _____ *congressman* _____

maid _____ *garbage man* _____

businessman _____

2. **Avoid unnecessary marking.** For example, if I am trying to explain to another student who Sky is, I might say, "Sky is the Native American, non-traditional-age student with a birthmark on her face, who sits in the last row." This description contains a whopping three markers which are most likely irrelevant to the identification of Sky.

    Discuss how and to whom the following markers might be unnecessary and/or offensive:

    a.   "I have an excellent Asian, woman doctor."

    _____

    b.   "I spoke to my mother's young, male nurse."

    _____

    c.   "You'd love my speech professor. She's a 53-year-old mouthy white woman, packing a few extra pounds, but the woman really knows how to give a lecture!"

    _____

    _____

    _____

3. **Avoid unnecessary associations.** For example: "My Interpersonal Communication professor, the recent recipient of a Fulbright Scholarship, asked me to turn in my paper on Friday."
    Spend the day listening for "unnecessary associations" and list them below:

    _____

    _____

    _____

E. Avoid racist labels by enlarging your knowledge base to reflect the contributions made by other racial and cultural groups.
    1.   Racism is embedded in our language system (Asante) and demonstrated by what people say about others.

2. Our language reflects the "knowledge system" we are taught. Columnist Andy Rooney once wrote, "While Indians have a grand past, the impact of their culture on the world has been slight. There are no great American Indian novels, no poetry. There's no memorable music." In what ways does Rooney's thought process represent a Eurocentric view of human events and achievements?

    _____

    _____

    _____

    _____

3. To combat racism and racist language, we must accurately learn the contributions that have been made by other racial and cultural groups. How easy is it for you to prove Rooney wrong? Can you list well-known Native American authors and cite their works? If not, why not?

    _____

    _____

    _____

4. It is the context of the words—the situation, the time, the feelings of the participants, the place, or the tone of voice—that causes damage.

When my daughter Kelly was in high school, she and other student council members, who attended a 99% Caucasian school, joined Native American high school students from a nearby reservation school, to discuss whether the Causacian high school should eliminate its use of a Native American logo. Caucasian students, angry about the possibility of losing the logo, called my daughter "Indian Lover." Have you had a similar experience where situation, feelings, place, and tone conveyed that the language was clearly racist?

Key Terms in Chapter 4
(Define each of the terms below.)

collectivistic cultures _____

_____

connotation _____

_____

dating generalizations _____

_____

denotation _____

_____

dialects _____

_____

gender _____

_____

generic language _____

_____

high-context communication _____

_____

high power-distance societies _____

_____

high uncertainty avoidance _____

_____

indexing generalizations _____

_____

individualistic cultures _____

_____

jargon _____

_____

language _____

_____

low-context communication _____

_____

low power-distance societies_____

_____

low uncertainty avoidance _____

_____

marking _____

_____

nonparallel language _____

_____

power distance _____

_____

sex _____

_____

slang _____

_____

speech community _____

_____

words _____

_____

Interesting Sites on the Internet

http://writingguide.geneseo.edu/conv.shtml
> SUNY Geneseo's Online Writing Guide offers the conventions of writing: how writing is conventional, avoiding sexist language, and avoiding racist language.

http://www.pride-unlimited.com/probono/idioms1.html
> This site is provided by Pride Unlimited and presents the meaning and origins of idioms and axioms currently used in America.

http://www.hcc.hawaii.edu/intranet/committees/FacDevCom/guidebk/teachtip/inclusiv.htm
> The Media Task Force of the Honolulu County Committee on the Status of Women provides numerous examples on degendering the English language to avoid derogatory language.

http://www.lamp.ac.uk/trs/essay_writing/appendix1.html
> The Department of Theology, Religious Studies & Islamic Studies at the University of Wales, Lampeter posts its 1999 guidelines for the use of inclusive language in essay writing.

http://www.yahooligans.com/reference/thesaurus/introduction.html
> This site provides information on a word's meaning as derived from its denotation and connotation, as well as what to be aware of when using a synonym in writing.

Exercise 4.1   Name _____

How Dare You Say *Niggardly*

Purpose:

1. To increase your awareness of connotative meanings of words.
2. To increase your awareness of the pain that accompanies certain words, depending upon life experiences.

Instructions:

A. Write down the denotative meaning of the word *niggardly*.
B. Read the background material listed below.
C. Surmise a connotative meaning of the word *niggardly* for the names listed.

_____

Background:

In January, 1999, a white mayoral aide in Washington, D.C., named David Howard was conversing with an African-American official concerning fiscal matters. During that conversation, Howard used the word *niggardly*. The African-American official took offense. Washington, D.C. mayor Anthony Williams accepted Howard's resignation. The mayor said that although Howard said nothing that was "in itself racist," using a word that could be so readily misunderstood was like "getting caught smoking in a refinery with a resulting explosion."

On February 1, 1999, U.W.-Madison student Amelia Rideau told members of the U.W.-Madison faculty "Speech Code" committee and the U.W. Faculty Senate about an incident in which a U.W.-Madison English literature professor used the word *niggardly* during a discussion of Chaucer's *Canterbury Tales*. She is said to have left the room in tears.

Attempt to surmise the "connotative" meaning of the word *niggardly* for the following:

1. David Howard _____

2. Anthony Williams _____

3. Amelia Rideau _____

4. U.W.-Madison English literature professor_____

   _____

5. The students in the literature class _____

   _____

6. African-American official _____

Exercise 4.2

Name _____

Red Hair and Freckles—I Can Spot
Someone Irish a Mile Away!

Purpose:
1. To increase awareness of the overuse of generalizations and stereotypes in everyday conversation.
2. To increase awareness of the role that indexing plays in effective communication.

Instructions:
A. Read the statements below.
B. Decide whether the statement is an appropriate use of generalization.
C. If not, "index" the statement so that it avoids stereotyping or over generalizing.

Statements:
1. "Native Americans avoid direct eye contact with people whom they respect. I'm certain that is why Aimee doesn't look at you." Is the statement appropriate? ____

   If not, index. _____

2. "Is it true that you drive an Acura? Great car! You can drive it for at least 300,000 miles." Is the statement appropriate? _____

   If not, index. _____

3. "Hey, Kevin. When did you get your nose pierced? Are you nuts? You're gonna have a million infections." Is the statement appropriate? _____

   If not, index. _____

4. "Beth, I saw the guy who asked you out. He's gorgeous. I could be wrong on this one, but I bet you will be perfect for each other." Is the statement appropriate? _____

   If not, index. _____

5. "Kristina, I heard that you are three months pregnant. You poor thing. You must be miserable with morning sickness." Is the statement appropriate? _____

   If not, index. _____

Exercise 4.3

Name _____

He Talks Like a Woman

Purpose: To increase your awareness of language patterns that women use which cause their language to be labeled "characteristically female."

Instructions:
A. Read the statements below.
B. Identify what portion of the statement "marks" it as one "characteristically female."

Statements:

1.   "Our Interpersonal Communication prof is very, very interesting!"

    Explanation: _____

    _____

2.   "His new haircut is attractive, isn't it?"

    Explanation: _____

    _____

3.   "I think you are a great friend."

    Explanation: _____

    _____

4.   "Thank you so much for the invitation."

    Explanation: _____

    _____

5.   "I wish I were a college professor."

    Explanation: _____

    _____

Exercise 4.4   Name _____

Would You Please Tell Our Waitress Steve
that We Are Ready to Order!

Purpose:
1. To create an awareness of words which conjure up male and female specific images.
2. To determine acceptable alternatives to gender specific words.

Instructions:
A. Divide class into pairs.
B. With your partner, look at the list of words/expressions below. Do not look at the list until the instructor says "Begin."
C. Your instructor will keep time as you and your partner attempt to identify one "gender neutral" alternative for each word/expression.
D. When you have completed the list, indicate so to your instructor and record your time.
E. With the class, discuss which words/expressions gave you the greatest trouble and why.
F. Discuss the "amount of time" it took for you and your partner to come up with gender neutral alternatives. Why do you think others were so much faster/slower than you?

Terms: Alternative:

1.   policeman   _____

2.   manhole cover   _____

3.   waitress   _____

4.   steward/stewardess   _____

5.   chairman   _____

6.   actress   _____

7.   businessman   _____

8.   "Sharon, would you please man the switchboard?"

      _____

9.   (to a mixed-gender class) "Hey, guys!" _____

10.   "All men are created equal."   _____

11.   "If a student were to miss class often, he would probably fail this class."

      _____

Exercise 4.5

He's a Snake

Purpose: To enhance your ability to appeal to the senses of others by backing up your concrete words with real life examples.

Instructions:
A. Identify the names of 5 people you know well.
B. Identify one "concrete" word that describes each individual.
C. Back up each concrete word with an example.
D. Share the example with a partner and see if your partner is able to identify the "concrete" word that you selected to describe the individual.

	Name	**Concrete Word**	**Example**
Person #1			
Person #2			
Person #3			
Person #4			
Person #5			

Exercise 4.6   Name _____

He's Raunchy! I Mean "Sexually Deviant"

Purpose: To enhance your ability to build a more precise or specific or concrete vocabulary through the process of mental brainstorming.

Instructions:
A. Ask your partner to describe the people/objects listed below using single words.
B. Then ask partner to pause and assess (mentally brainstorm) whether a different word might be more precise.
C. Record partner's first word and second word (if given).
D. Examine the first word and the second word to determine whether the process of mental brainstorming resulted in a more precise descriptor.

DESCRIBE IT FAST

	First Word	**Second Word**
Instructor for this class		
Best friend		
Your car		
Your living accommodations		
Your wardrobe		
Your hair		
Your personality		
Your pet peeve		
Most important quality in opposite sex		
This class		

SELF EXAMINATION – CHAPTER 4

True/False   If false, explain what is wrong with the statement.

___ 1. Concrete words appeal to our senses by using real life examples.

_____

___ 2. In low-context communication, meaning is in the message.

_____

___ 3. Low uncertainty avoidance cultures are intolerant of differing behaviors and opinions.

_____

___ 4. Mental brainstorming is a critical, evaluative process of generating alternatives.

_____

___ 5. Connotative meanings are standard dictionary meanings.

_____

Multiple Choice

___ 6. Which of the following is the BEST example of a dated message?
   A.   It rained every day that I was in Europe.
   B.   I loved the "Intelligent Blond" joke she told in class yesterday.
   C.   I enjoyed class yesterday.
   D.   I didn't understand anything my French professor said.

___ 7. Which of the following is NOT characteristic of a collectivistic culture?
   A.   Use high-context communication.
   B.   Others are expected to know what you are saying.
   C.   The messages are presented directly.
   D.   Group goals are emphasized.

___ 8. Which of the following is NOT true of denotative meanings?
   A.   Meanings change over time.
   B.   Meanings reflect current and past practice.
   C.   Meanings vary depending upon life experiences.
   D.   Use words to define words.

___ 9. Which of the following is an example of an indexed generalization?
   A.   "Last March, when I was in Florida, it rained every day."
   B.   "She's a woman, isn't she? I could be wrong, but I bet she'll love the flowers."
   C.   "He's a jock. Of course he watches the sports channel."
   D.   "Paris is the most beautiful city in the world. You will never want to leave.

___10. Which of the following is NOT true about the language of women?
    A.   Women tend to ask more questions than men.
    B.   Women tend to use more intensifiers than men.
    C.   Women tend to be rated as having less dynamism than men.
    D.   Women tend to be rated as having lower social status than men.

Complete the Thought

11.   In the phrase "Alex, the old man sitting next to Naomi" the words *old man* are an example of _____.

12.   In the phrase "All men are created equal" the word *men* is an example of language known as _____.

Essay Questions

13.   As we attempt to make our own language more appropriate, Verderber and Verderber ask that we avoid five specific usages that others perceive as offensive. List and explain.

14.   Dale, a senior majoring in Communication, has been invited to attend a faculty colloquium. Upon entering the room where the colloquium is being held, he sees the professor who invited him. He says, "Hey, man, sorry I'm late. I was hangin' with friends. I forgot my damn watch so I was clueless about the time." Dale has violated the three strategies that Verderber and Verderber highlight for crafting appropriate verbal messages. Explain.

Interpersonal Problem Solver

One of your classmates comes from a "masculine culture." She is a talented athlete who was a "walk-on" at tryouts for the women's basketball team. The coach just notified her that she made the team. Based upon your understanding of cultural adherence to traditional sex roles, what reaction might she anticipate from her extended family?

Chapter 5:   Communicating Through Nonverbal Behaviors

Interactive Chapter Outline

I.   Nonverbal communication behaviors are actions, vocal qualities, and activities that typically accompany a verbal message.

  A.   These behaviors are usually interpreted as intentional.

  B.   These behaviors have agreed-upon interpretations in the culture or speech community.

  C.   These behaviors are used as a guide to the nature and depth of our feelings.

II.   Kinesics, the technical name for the study of body motions used in communication, includes four major body motions.

  A.   Eye contact, sometimes referred to as gaze, involves looking directly at the person or persons with whom we are communicating.
    1.   Eye contact allows us to tell when the other is paying attention.
    2.   Talkers maintain eye contact approximately 40 percent of the time.
    3.   Listeners maintain eye contact approximately 70 percent of the time.
    4.   We maintain more eye contact when we are discussing topics with which we are comfortable and less with uncomfortable topics. Be aware of eye contact during your next conversation and explain the following:

            Were you the talker or listener? _____

            What percent of eye contact did you and the other maintain? _____

            What was your degree of comfort with the topic? _____

  B.   Facial expression is the arrangement of facial muscles to communicate emotional states or reactions to messages.
    1.   Facial expression muscles include the brow and forehead, eyes, eyelids and root of nose, cheeks, mouth, remainder of nose and chin.
    2.   Facial expressions mirror thoughts and feelings but, at times, fail to match feelings and meaning. Has someone asked you what was wrong when you were feeling fine? Does it happen frequently? If yes, why?

            _____

            _____

C.   Six basic emotions recognized across cultures include happiness, sadness, surprise, fear, anger, and disgust.

D.   Gestures are movements of hands, arms, and fingers that we use to describe or emphasize.
   1.   We expect gestures to accompany verbal meaning.
   2.   Problems arrive when gestures do not reinforce, but contradict, meaning. Try sending a "no" gesture to someone when your words say "yes." Describe the reaction.

   _____

   _____

E.   Posture is the position and movement of the body.
   1.   Changes in posture communicate.
   2.   Sitting up and forward communicates increased attention. As you are listening to someone, lean forward. Do you notice a reaction?

   _____

III.   Body motions communicate in specific ways.

A.   Emblems are nonverbal gestures that take the place of words or phrases.
   1.   Sign language is based entirely on the use of emblems.
   2.   Emblems have the power to control. Identify the nonverbal behavior someone recently used in an attempt to control your behavior.

   _____

   _____

B.   Illustrators are nonverbal gestures that complement a speaker's words.
   1.   Gestures emphasize, show direction of thought, show position, describe, and mimic.
   2.   Gestures used inappropriately detract from meaning. Try using huge gestures in a one-on-one conversation. Describe the reaction of the listener.

   _____

   _____

C.   Affect displays are facial expressions and gestures that augment the verbal expression of feelings.
   1.   Affect displays are automatic. For example, a paper cut is likely to result in some display of facial expression.
   2.   People differ in the way they display feelings so care must be taken in forming conclusions. Are you someone who plays down affect displays

of pain? Do you know someone who magnifies affect displays?
Explain.

_____

_____

    D.   Regulators are facial expressions or gestures used to control or regulate the flow of a conversation.

        1.   Listeners emit nonverbal behaviors that tell the speaker what to do. A nod, a wince, a lifted brow speak to us. During a lecture, make a conscious effort to emit a nonverbal sign of confusion to your professor. See if he/she reacts.

        2.   Effective communicators respond to regulators. Identify one regulating behavior that you saw directed your way today. How did you respond?

_____

_____

    E.   Adaptors are gestures used to relieve tension. I crack my knuckles. What do you do?

_____

IV.   Cultural differences in body motions are well documented.

    A.   Cultures vary in use of direct eye contact.

        1.   Japanese direct their gaze around the Adam's apple, not the others' eyes.

        2.   Chinese, Indonesians, and rural Mexicans lower eyes as a sign of deference.

        3.   Arabs look intently for long periods to demonstrate interest.

        4.   African Americans use more eye contact than European Americans when speaking and less when listening. What cultural differences in eye contact have you observed?

_____

_____

    B.   Cultures vary in use of gestures, movements, and facial expressions.

        1.   Different cultures use similar gestures to convey totally different meanings. Can you identify a European American gesture that got President Nixon in trouble? Do you know how a French person gestures "one"? Can you offer other cultural examples where similar gestures convey different meanings?

_____

_____

_____

2. Displays of emotion vary from culture to culture. Have you experienced the de-intensified emotional behavior cues of Eastern cultures? Explain.

_____

_____

V. Men and women show differences in nonverbal communication behaviors.

A. Women in the United States have more frequent eye contact than men and hold contact longer.

B. Women smile more than men, but their smiles are harder to interpret.

C. Men's smiles generally express positive feelings. Women's smiles tend to be responses to affiliation and friendliness.

D. Gestures used by women are profoundly different from those used by men. Examine the gestures below. Based upon your sex, do you agree that you fit this description? If not, have you experienced "gender teasing"? Explain.
   1. Women keep arms closer to body than men.
   2. Women are less likely to lean forward with body.
   3. Women play more with hair or clothing.
   4. Women tap their hands more than men.

_____

_____

_____

VI. Men and women differ in their interpretation of nonverbal communication behaviors of others.

A. Women are better than men at decoding nonverbal vocal and facial cues.

B. Men seem less sensitive in interpreting women's nonverbal behaviors. In your relationships with the "opposite sex" have you found this to be true? Has it caused problems in the relationship? Explain.

_____

_____

_____

VII. Paralanguage, or vocalics, is the nonverbal "sound" of what we hear, governed by four major vocal characteristics.

A.   Pitch is the highness or lowness of tone. Nerves cause pitch to rise. Describe your pitch. So high you squeak? So low you growl?

_____

B.   Volume is the loudness or softness of tone. Describe your natural volume. Is it so soft that others are repeatedly asking you to speak up? So loud that you don't need a microphone? Why?

_____

_____

C.   Rate is the speed at which a person speaks. Identify your rate.

_____

D.   Quality is the sound of the voice.   Record your voice. Then listen to it. Do you like what you hear? If not, why not? What would you like to change? How do you plan to change it?

_____

_____

VIII.   Vocal interferences, extraneous sounds or words, interrupt fluent speech.

A.   Interferences prevent listeners from concentrating. My interference word is *okay*. What is yours?

_____

B.   Interferences mark places or fill in gaps. I use *uh*. What do you use?

_____

C.   Some speakers use so many interference words that the message is unintelligible. In your next conversation, try to notice what interferences the other speaker uses. Identify those interferences below. Did they affect communication? Repeat this exercise, but now identify your interferences. Did they affect communication? Do you want to get rid of your interferences? Do you have a plan?

_____

_____

_____

_____

_____

IX.   People learn about us and judge us based upon self-presentation.

A. Choice of clothing and personal grooming communicate.
    1. We express individuality and communicate political feelings in our dress
        and personal grooming. Analyze your wardrobe. What does it say
        about you?

    _____

    _____

    _____

    2. We create barriers. Recently I heard a father describe his daughter's
        poor choice in boyfriends. He said, "He didn't wear a gold necklace so
        how was I to know he was a drug dealer?" The irony was that, as the
        father spoke, he was wearing a small gold chain around his neck. Does
        your clothing create barriers? With whom? Why? Would you like to
        change? How?

    _____

    _____

    _____

B. Poise refers to assurance of manner.
    1. Twenty percent of the population is extremely nervous when
        encountering strangers and speaking before groups.
    2. Nervousness decreases with confidence. Think back to when you were
        near someone new whom you found attractive. How poised/nervous
        were you? Why? How did your nervousness affect communication?

    _____

    _____

C. Touch, putting a hand or finger in contact with another, is considered the most
    basic form of conversation.
    1. How we touch can convey power, empathy, and understanding. Has
        someone touched you recently? What message do you believe he/she
        was conveying with the touch? What was your reaction to being
        touched?

    _____

    _____

    _____

2. Women tend to touch less than men but value it more. Are you someone who touches during conversations? Why? How do others react to your touching?

_____

_____

_____

3. Women view touch as a demonstration of warmth and affiliation where men view it as instrumental; with women touch is a prelude to sexual activity. How do you react when touched by a stranger to whom you are attracted?

_____

_____

4. Appropriateness of touch differs with context. Consider your touching behavior. Can you recall a time when someone touched you inappropriately? What was the context? What did you say or do?

_____

_____

D. How we manage and react to others' use and management of informal time is another way in which we self-present.
    1. Duration of time is the amount of time we regard as appropriate for certain events and activities. When an instructor exceeds class time limits with his/her lecture, how do you react?

_____

2. Timing of an activity determines how we regard others or how others regard us. Do you do things at times that your friends find "strange"? Explain. My in-laws eat dinner at 4 p.m. When do you eat? Why?

_____

_____

_____

E. Punctuality is the extent to which one adheres strictly to appointed or regular time. Which of the following tends to describe you: "on time," "always early," "always late"? Why?

_____

_____

X. Self-presentation behaviors differ in meanings assigned depending upon the culture.

A.   Touch differences are highly correlated with culture. In high-contact cultures (Latin America and Mediterranean) close is positive and far is negative. Low-contact cultures (Asian) hold the reverse to be true. Northern European cultures fall into the medium to low-contact range.

B.   Time is viewed monochronically (one-dimensional) in some cultures (U.S.), a scarce resource meant to be spent or saved. Other cultures (Asian, Latin American, Middle Eastern) view time polychronically, where the word *late* has no meaning. I've given lectures at a Native American tribal college where most students are polychronic. As a monochrone, I used to go crazy when students arrived at all different stages of the lecture. Now, I anticipate late arrivals. Have you had a similar experience? Explain.

_____

_____

XI.   We communicate nonverbally through how we manage the physical environment in which our conversations occur.

A.   We choose living space to fit our lifestyle. I live alone in a four-bedroom home. Consider your apartment/home. What does your choice of living space say about you?

_____

B.   Movable objects are moved in that space to create a desired atmosphere. In my daughter Kelly's living room, all of her furniture faces the television. It drives me crazy. I offered to help her arrange the furniture in a way that was more conducive to conversation. She smiled and said, "No thanks, Mom. My friends and I like it this way." Ouch! Does your furniture encourage/discourage discussion? Explain.

_____

_____

C.   The use of space is one index of how people are going to treat you and how they expect you to treat them. Think about a "space" where you feel most comfortable. Explain why.

_____

_____

D.   Proxemics, the study of informal space around the place we are occupying at the time, is determined by our culture.
    1.   Intimate distance in the U.S. culture, up to eighteen inches, is appropriate for private conversations with close friends.
    2.   Personal distance, from eighteen inches to four feet, is where casual conversations occur.

3. Social distance, from four to twelve feet, is where impersonal business occurs.

4. Public distance is anything more than twelve feet. Think back to a conversation you recently experienced that violated one of the rules of distance (expectancy violation theory). How did you feel about the person who violated the rule? How did you feel about the actual violation? Did you say or do anything? Why? Have you ever experienced a space violation that you construed as sexual harassment? If yes, explain how you handled it.

_____

_____

_____

_____

5. Territory is the space over which we claim ownership, whether or not we are currently occupying it. When someone moves into our territory, we feel resentful. My colleague recently sat in a chair "marked" for another person. Her intention was to usurp his power and provoke a reaction. Wow, did it! Have you had a similar experience? Explain. What territory do you mark as "yours"?

_____

_____

_____

E. Temperature, lighting, and color affect communication.

1. Temperature can stimulate or inhibit effective communication. During Wisconsin winters, every room in my house is freezing except for the family room. My friends head directly to that room.

2. Lighting adds meaning. In the family room, I keep the lights low. Some friends turn up the lights as they enter the room. Are you a bright or low light communicator? Why?

_____

_____

3. Color stimulates emotion and physical reactions. Think of your favorite place to be. What role do colors, lighting, and temperature play in making it your favorite place? What are your favorite colors? Do you know why?

_____

_____

Key Terms in Chapter 5
(Define each of the terms below.)

activity _____

_____

adaptors _____

_____

affect displays _____

_____

color _____

_____

duration _____

_____

emblems _____

_____

eye contact _____

_____

facial expression _____

_____

gestures _____

_____

illustrators _____

_____

lighting _____

_____

monochronic _____

_____

nonverbal communication behaviors _____

_____

paralanguage _____

_____

pitch _____

_____

poise _____

_____

polychronic _____

_____

posture _____

_____

proxemics _____

_____

punctuality _____

_____

quality _____

_____

rate _____

_____

regulators _____

_____

temperature _____

_____

territory _____

_____

touch _____

_____

vocalics _____

_____

vocal interferences _____

_____

volume _____

_____

Exercise 5.1   Name _____

Is That Love I See?

Purpose:
1. To enhance your ability to encode and decode nonverbal communication behaviors.
2. To test the hypothesis that women are better than men in interpreting nonverbal behaviors.

Instructions:
A. Pair up with another student of the opposite sex.
B. One partner will take List A and the other List B.
C. Briefly rehearse nonverbal behaviors that accompany each word.
D. Choose words, in random order, from the list and use nonverbal behaviors to express them. Keep track of how many attempts your partner makes before correctly labeling the emotion.
E. Discuss with your partner why you had difficulties identifying certain words.
F. Identify how many total tries the male made and how many total tries the female made.

List A	**List B**
1. happiness	1. frustration
2. concern	2. pain
3. sadness	3. job
4. frustration	4. confusion
5. delight	5. wonder
6. anger	6. disbelief
7. fatigue	7. passion
8. curiosity	8. affection
9. pain	9. anxiety
10. aloofness	10. understanding

Exercise 5.2   Name _____

Just Point Me in the Right Direction

Purpose: To convey an understanding of the role that nonverbal behavior plays in both encoding and decoding messages.

Instructions:
A. With a partner, decide who is partner A and who is partner B.
B. Partner A is sighted. Partner B has, since birth, been unable to see.
C. Partner A must verbally direct partner B from where he/she presently is to the outside of the building. Place blindfold over eyes of partner B and walk a ways behind him/her. Partner B can say nothing.
D. After you have reached your destination, return to the classroom and discuss what partner A did or did not do to clearly communicate.
E. Discuss how nonverbal behavior would have helped.

_____

Discussion:

Reaction to Partner's Directions:

Reaction to No Nonverbals:

Exercise 5.3   Name _____

Look Me In The Eye

Purpose: To convey an understanding of the important role that eye contact plays in the expression of interest.

Instructions:
A. Over the next few days, enter into five 5-minute conversations with friends.
B. The average U.S. listener looks at speaker about 70% of the time. Look at speaker about 20% of the time. Watch everyone who passes by. Read the paper. Do as much as possible to not look at the speaker.
C. After 5 minutes, tell the speaker what you were doing. Ask the speaker how your lack of eye contact made him/her feel. (Hopefully, you won't lose friends during this exercise.)

_____

Speaker #1 Reaction:

Speaker #2 Reaction:

Speaker #3 Reaction:

Speaker #4 Reaction:

Speaker #5 Reaction:

Exercise 5.4   Name _____

Are You Watching?

Purpose:
1. To convey an understanding of the role that "regulators" play in controlling the flow of a conversation.
2. To enhance your ability to encode accurate facial messages.

Instructions:
A. Practice nonverbal behaviors for the following emotions: (1) confusion, (2) pleasure, (3) disagreement, (4) disgust, (5) pain.
B. Throughout the next week, find appropriate places to use the nonverbal behaviors. Keep using the nonverbal behavior until someone responds "supportively." For example, if you are confused in class, show it. See how long it takes your instructor to ask, "What's wrong?"

---

1.   Confusion:
      Where used?
      How long to notice?
      What did he/she say?

2.   Pleasure:
      Where used?
      How long to notice?
      What did he/she say?

3.   Disagreement:
      Where used?
      How long to notice?
      What did he/she say?

4.   Disgust:
      Where used?
      How long to notice?
      What did he/she say?

5.   Pain:
      Where used?
      How long to notice?
      What did he/she say?

Exercise 5.5   Name _____

You Have the Most Incredible Eyes!

Purpose: To create an awareness of the role that "gaze" plays in conveying interest in the opposite sex.

Instructions:

A. Organize a "night out," at a busy university spot with a friend of the same sex.
B. For the first half of the evening, you and your friend will attempt to gain the attention of 4 people of the opposite sex through use of eye contact. When you gain his/her attention, smile and continue your gaze until he/she looks away or responds.
C. For the second half of the evening, you and your friend will attempt to gain the attention of 4 people of the opposite sex through use of eye contact. But, when you gain his/her attention, immediately look away.
D. Discuss your results with the class.

SUSTAINED GAZE	RECORD THEIR RESPONSES
Person #1	
Person #2	
Person #3	
Person #4	
AVERTED GAZE	**RECORD THEIR RESPONSES**
Person #1	
Person #2	
Person #3	
Person #4	

Exercise 5.6

Name _____

Move Over, Man, You're Suffocating Me!

Purpose: To increase awareness of the role that space plays in maintaining a level of personal comfort.

Instructions:
A. Go to the library and find a table where only one person (someone that you don't know) is seated.
B. Sit in the chair immediately next to the person, placing your chair as close as possible (within 8 inches) so that you have invaded his/her intimate space.
C. Remain there for five minutes.
D. Record the nonverbal reactions of the person whose territory you have invaded.
E. Repeat this exercise at a local coffee shop and at the Student Union.
F. Discuss the results of this exercise with students in class.

Record nonverbal responses. (Did the individual appear resentful of the fact that you had invaded his/her territory? If yes, how did he/she express that resentment?)

Library:

Coffee Shop:

Student Union:

SELF EXAMINATION – CHAPTER 5

True/False   If false, explain what is wrong with the statement.

___1. Women in the U.S. tend to hold eye contact longer than men.

_____

___2. Emblems are nonverbal gestures that take the place of words or phrases.

_____

___3. Kinesics is the technical name for the study of body motions used in communication.

_____

___4. The smiles of men generally express more positive feelings than the smiles of women.

_____

___5. In the U.S. listeners maintain eye contact approximately 40 percent of the time.

_____

Multiple Choice

___6. Which of the following is NOT true concerning the gestures of women and men?
  A.   Women keep their arms further away from the body than men.
  B.   Women are less likely to lean forward with body than men.
  C.   Women play more with hair or clothing than men.
  D.   Women tap their hands more than men.

___7. The word *okay* is an example of which of the following?
  A.   paralanguage   C.   interference
  B.   vocalics   D.   regulator

___8. Six basic emotions are recognized across cultures. Which of the following is NOT one of the six?
  A.   surprise   B.   disgust   C.   confusion   D.   sadness

___9. Which of the following is NOT a well documented cultural difference?
  A.   Japanese direct their gaze around the Adam's apple.
  B.   Chinese lower eyes as a sign of deference.
  C.   Arabs look intently for long periods to demonstrate interest.
  D.   African Americans use less eye contact than European Americans when speaking.

___10. Talkers maintain eye contact approximately what percent of the time?

     A.   40%   B.   50%   C.   60%   D.   70%

Complete the Thought

11.   A culture that views time as a scarce resource meant to be spent is referred to as

_____

12.   The study of informal space around the place we are occupying at the time is

_____

Essay Questions

13.   Cultural differences in body motions are well documented. Explain.

14.   People learn about us and judge us based upon four aspects of self-presentation. Explain.

Interpersonal Problem Solver

You just received news that you are the recipient of a major scholarship. You would love to shout it from the rooftop but are afraid of sounding egotistical. You just wish your friends would ask. Based upon your understanding of kinesics and paralanguage, what can you do to get other people to say, "What's up?"

Interesting Sites on the Internet

http://members.aol.com/doder1/proxemi1.htm
> David Givens, of the Center for Nonverbal Studies, discusses proxemics, what Edward T. Hall called the study of humankind's perception and use of space.

http://www.cpsr.org/cpsr/gender/mulvaney.txt
> This site presents "Gender Differences in Communication: An Intercultural Experience," written by Becky Mulvaney of Florida Atlantic University.

http://www.presentersuniversity.com/courses/show_archive.cfm?RecordID=39
> This site, sponsored by InFocus Corporation, discusses The Power of Body Language from "Gestures: Your Body Speaks" published by Toastmasters International.

http://members.aol.com/nonverbal2/nvcom.htm
> David Givens, Center for Nonverbal Studies, presents a melange of statistics and conjecture concerning the role of nonverbal communication in our lives.

http://www.sirc.org/publik/flirt.html
> This site, sponsored by the Social Issues Research Centre in Oxford, England, presents the SIRC Guide to Flirting: What Social Science can tell you about it and how to do it.

Chapter 6:   Holding Effective Conversations

Interactive Chapter Outline

I.   Conversations, informal interchanges of thoughts and feelings distinguished by an equal distribution of speaker rights, have three primary characteristics.

      A.   A conversation is fully interactive. At least two people take turns exchanging messages.

      B.   Conversation is locally managed. Those involved set the rules.

      C.   Topics are mundane, commonplace, and practical. Think of your most recent conversation. Describe the conversation by focusing on the three primary characteristics. In your opinion, does a dialogue on whether or not the U.S. should outlaw the death penalty fit under the category of "mundane"? Explain.

           _____

           _____

           _____

II.   Conversations can be viewed from two different perspectives.

      A.   Some conversations fill a need (goals perspective). If you are upset with a friend and desire to mend the relationship, a conversation may fill that need. Describe a recent goals perspective conversation.

           _____

           _____

           _____

      B.   Some conversations build relationships (relational perspective). Describe a recent conversation that made you feel good about your relationship.

           _____

           _____

           _____

III.   Conversations have structure.

      A.   Casual social conversations are spontaneous with no planned agenda.
           1.   The topic is introduced and accepted or rejected.

2. The accepted topic is discussed until participants believe it is played out. In your next social conversation, make a mental note of topics introduced and accepted or rejected. Were any of the rejected topics yours? How did you feel?

_____

_____

B. Pragmatic problem-consideration conversations include at least one participant with a goal.
    1. Begin with a greeting and small talk.
    2. One person initiates a topic that requires deliberation.
    3. Information is exchanged and processed.
    4. Decisions are summarized and next steps are clarified.
    5. A formal closing allows participants to move to a social conversation.

Describe your most recent pragmatic problem-consideration conversation. Did it conclude with Step 5? How important do you believe Step 5 to be?

_____

_____

IV. Conversations have rules that may differ depending upon the group.

A. Rules must allow for choice as to whether or not they will be followed. You can choose to interrupt me before I finish speaking.

B. Rules are prescriptive. You may be criticized for not following a rule. Have you ever been told by a friend, "Stop interrupting me"?

C. Rules are contextual. They may or may not be applicable, depending upon the communication situation. Do you whisper in church? Do you use the f-word with parents? Romantic interest? Friends?

_____

_____

D. Rules specify appropriate human behavior. What would happen if your professor stuck her/his tongue out at you in class?

_____

Discuss the observance of these rules in your most recent conversation. Which rules were broken? Which rules were observed? How?

_____

_____

_____

V.   Successful conversations observe six maxims.

    A.   The quality maxim calls for truthful information.

    B.   The quantity maxim calls for enough, but not too much, information.

    C.   The relevancy maxim calls for information that is on topic.

    D.   The manner maxim calls for specific, organized communication of thoughts.

    E.   The morality maxim calls for moral/ethical speech.

    F.   The politeness maxim calls for us to be courteous.
        1.   One cultural form of politeness is accommodation: the courteous submission or acquiescence to opinions, wishes, or judgment of another.
        2.   Another form of politeness is topic shifting. Describe a recent "heated" conversation where you employed accommodation or topic shifting in an attempt to reduce the heat. Did it reduce the heat? Explain.

_____

_____

_____

VI.   We can improve conversational effectiveness.

    A.   Effective conversationalists have knowledge about a wide range of topics. How well would you do with the following topics: Existentialism? U.S. politics? Cloning? Develop a list of topics about which you are knowledgeable.

_____

_____

_____

_____

    B.   Effective conversationalists provide free information, extra material that the responder can use. Question: "Do you like to ski?" Answer: "Not really, but I try. I've fallen more than I care to remember." Try responding to this question by providing free information: "Have you ever wanted to climb Mt. Everest?"

_____

_____

C.   Effective conversationalists ask questions that are likely to motivate responses. What might be wrong with this question? Speaker: "I have two roommates." Questioner: "Are you romantically involved with either?"

_____

How quick are you to avoid answering personal questions of strangers? Why?

_____

_____

D.   Effective conversationalists credit sources. Complimenting the person from whom you have gathered information allows the listener to evaluate the quality of your information and makes the person whose idea you are citing feel better. "Naomi, I think you said this at an earlier meeting . . . ."

E.   Effective conversationalists balance speaking and listening. Do you tend to dominate conversations?
    1.   Take turns. Help those who are having trouble entering the conversation. Pull back if you are speaking too much.
    2.   Speak an appropriate length of time. Avoid extremes like one-word answers and full-blown monologues.
    3.   Recognize and heed turn-exchanging cues and beware of unintentional cues.
        a.   Lowering volume and pitch says "next."
        b.   Lowering head says "next."
        c.   Pause says "next."
    4.   Use and comply with conversation-directing behavior. "Tamika, do you agree?"
    5.   Minimize interruptions and make sure that interruptions are appropriate.
        a.   Clarification and agreement interruptions are acceptable.
        b.   Interruptions that change topic or minimize contributions are likely to be viewed as impolite.

In your next conversation, try to put the five rules for effective conversation balance into practice. Explain the results. Which steps were easiest for you to employ? Why? Which were most challenging? Why?

_____

_____

_____

_____

_____

_____

F. Effective conversationalists maintain conversational coherence by making sure comments relate to those previously made by others.
    1. Give the speaker your full attention. Think of a conversation partner who does not give you full attention. How does it make you feel?
    2. Relate what you want to say to what others have said. Think of a conversation partner who does not pick up on what you have said. How does it make you feel?

    _____

    _____

G. Effective conversationalists express politeness by relating to others in ways that meet their face need: need to be appreciated and protected (Brown and Levinson's Politeness Theory).
    1. Express positive politeness. Respect the desire of others to be appreciated and approved (positive face). These statements express concern, compliments, and respectful titles of address.
    2. Express negative politeness. Statements recognize that you are imposing or intruding. They include: "I'm sorry for bothering you, but . . . ." Describe a recent conversation in which you used both positive and negative politeness.

    _____

    _____

    _____

    3. Consider potential problems that could result from face threatening acts and choose one of the strategies listed below based upon the following questions: How well do you know each other?
                                                                                                What power does the hearer have over you?
                                                                                                What risk is there of hurting the other person?
        Strategies:
        a. Deliver the face threatening act openly without consideration for politeness.
        b. Deliver the face threatening act with some form of positive politeness reducing potential for loss of face.
        c. Deliver the face threatening act with negative politeness acknowledging that you may be imposing.
        d. Deliver the face threatening act indirectly or off the record allowing for the other person to pursue the issue if he/she chooses.
        e. Say nothing.

        Think of a recent face threatening conversation in which you were involved. Which of the above strategies did you use? How was your message received? Why? Do you think another strategy would have worked better? Which one? Why?

_____

_____

_____

_____

H.   Effective conversationalists engage in ethical dialogue.

An ethical conversationalist:
1.   Is authentic: if in disagreement, says so.
2.   Is empathetic: is able to imagine from the other person's point of view.
3.   Is confirming: expresses nonpossessive warmth.
4.   Demonstrates presentness, a willingness to listen actively.
5.   Treats conversational partners as equals.
6.   Is supportive, communicating praise of worthwhile efforts.

Think of your most recent conversation in which you expressed disagreement with the other person. Were your words well received? Why?

_____

In which aspects of ethical dialogue were you the weakest? Strongest?

_____

_____

VII.   The conversations of low-context cultures follow guidelines that differ from high-context cultures.

A.   Low-context communicators are more likely to include categorical words like "absolutely" and "positively." High-context communicators are more likely to use qualifiers like "maybe" and "perhaps."

B.   Low-context communicators follow the relevancy maxim using comments that are directly to the point. High-context communicators are more indirect and depend upon a receiver's sensitivity to nonverbal cues.

C.   Low-context communicators speak their mind and tell the truth. High-context communicators strive for harmony.

D.   Low-context communicators do not consider silence as good. High-context communicators use silence to express a variety of sentiments ranging from truthfulness to embarrassment to disagreement.

Depending upon whether you are a low-context or high-context communicator, describe communication problems that you have experienced with someone from the "other" culture.

_____

_____

_____

VIII. *Inter-Action Dialogue:* Conversations tend to follow unwritten rules. Read the dialogue between Susan and Sarah that appears in your text following the chapter summary. Before reading the analysis in the right-hand column, jot down some notes about the effectiveness of their conversation, using the following list of maxims and skills as your guide:

A. Effective conversations adhere to the following maxims:
   1. Quality
   2. Quantity
   3. Relevancy
   4. Manner
   5. Morality
   6. Politeness

B. Effective conversations require specific skills:
   1. Asking questions
   2. Providing free information
   3. Crediting sources
   4. Taking turns

In your opinion, did Susan sound as though she sincerely cared about Sarah? Did her reference to "hotties" sound appropriate? Sensitive? Did turn taking seem appropriate? When Susan discussed how lucky she was that her parents wouldn't let her go out with anyone who wasn't Jewish, was this relevant? Polite? Caring? Did Sarah seem to become defensive? Is Susan the type of person to whom you would feel comfortable speaking? Explain.

_____

_____

_____

_____

_____

Key Terms in Chapter 6
(Define each of the terms below.)

authenticity _____

_____

contextual rules _____

_____

conversational coherence _____

_____

cooperative principle _____

_____

empathy _____

_____

face-threatening acts _____

_____

free information _____

_____

goals perspective _____

_____

manner maxim _____

_____

morality maxim _____

_____

negative politeness _____

_____

politeness maxim _____

_____

positive politeness _____

_____

pragmatic problem-consideration conversations _____

_____

prescriptive rules _____

_____

presentness _____

_____

quality maxim _____

_____

quantity maxim _____

_____

relational perspective _____

_____

relevancy maxim _____

_____

supportive climate _____

_____

Interesting Sites on the Internet

http://www.mhnet.org/psyhelp/chap13/chap13o.htm
> Sponsored by Mental Health Net, this site presents five steps to follow for rational decision-making and problem-solving. Research is from Clayton Tucker-Ladd's book *Psychological Self-Help*.

http://www.implementer.com/implementer/web/step4_c/persuade-decrational.htm
> This site discusses how to make a "perfect" decision using a rational, seven-step decision-making method and also provides a more realistic method.

http://www.ku.edu/ ~ cte/resources/teachingtips/probsolving.html
> Sponsored by the University of Kansas Center for Teaching Excellence, this site provides suggestions for teaching problem-solving.

http://www.shinnova.com/part/99-japa/abj17-e.htm
> This site offers insight into the meaning behind the nonverbal communication of the Japanese.

http://www.collegegrad.com/jobsearch/15-7.shtml
> Sponsored by CollegeGrad.com, this site presents tips on how to use the top five nonverbals successfully in the interview process.

Exercise 6.1   Name _____

We Need to Talk

Purpose: To increase awareness of ways to avoid loss of face.

Instructions: Effective conversationalists express politeness by relating to others in ways that meet their face needs. Read the statements below and respond to the questions.
A. What form of politeness was used by the speaker?
B. How well do the two appear to know each other?
C. What is the perceived power relationship?
D. What is the perceived risk of hurting?

Paul is dean at the same university where the speaker, Mary, is a professor. Mary is upset with something Paul said at a recent meeting.
1. "Hey, Paul, sit down. We need to talk!"
2. "Paul, do you have a minute? I need to talk to you."
3. "Damn it all, Paul, can't you give me a minute of your precious time?"
4. "Paul, I think your speech at convocation was provocative. I always value what you have to say. By the way, if you have a moment, I'd really like to speak to you."
5. "Paul, I know how busy you are, and I really hate to bother you, but could I speak to you when it is convenient for you?"
6. Mary sees Paul in the hallway, hoping he will notice that she has something to say. He looks at her. She hesitates and then says, "Paul." He says, "Is something bothering you?"
7. Mary sees Paul in the hallway. She considers talking to him. She pauses and then keeps walking.

	Form of politeness used by speaker	How well they know each other	Perceived power relationship	Perceived risk of hurting
#1				
#2				
#3				
#4				
#5				
#6				
#7				

Exercise 6.2   Name _____

I've Got a Problem

Purpose: To increase your ability to engage in pragmatic problem-consideration conversations.

Instructions:
A. Identify a problem that you would like some help solving.
B. Identify one person with whom you feel comfortable addressing the problem.
C. Observe the following pragmatic problem-consideration conversation steps:
   1. Begin with a greeting and small talk.
   2. Initiate the topic that requires deliberation.
   3. Exchange and process the information.
   4. Summarize the decision and clarify the next step.
   5. Formally "end" the problem-consideration conversation and move into a social conversation.
D. Discuss with a partner how useful the 5-step process was. How important do you believe Step 1 and Step 5 are in the problem-consideration process? Are you someone who prefers to get "right to the problem?" Do you see where this process might have its strengths? Explain.

Discussion:

Exercise 6.3   Name _____

I Never Know What to Say

Purpose: To increase your awareness of the conversational effectiveness or
ineffectiveness of others.

Instructions:

A. Effective conversationalists have a bag of tricks. Together with a partner, study the
following list of tricks well enough to be able to identify them in a conversation:
A good conversationalist . . .
1. Is equipped with information on a wide range of topics.
2. Is willing to offer "extra" information when questions are asked.
3. Asks questions.
4. Balances speaking and listening.
5. Uses conversational directors like "Don't you agree?" or "What do you think?" which
draw the other person into the conversation.
6. Keeps interruptions at a minimum.
7. Makes sure that comments relate to previous comments by others.
8. Is polite.
9. Is ethical, authentic, empathetic, supportive, confirming, an active listener, and treats
as equals.
B. Engage in a conversation with your partner.
C. Complete the *Conversation Effectiveness Evaluation* on the next page.
D. Discuss the results with your partner. Do you agree with the ratings given? Discuss your
strong and weak areas. Discuss the evaluation form. Do you think that it is a useful gauge
in determining strong conversational skills?

Discussion:

CONVERSATIONAL EFFECTIVENESS EVALUATION

Rate your conversation partner using the following scale:

1	2	3	4	5	6	7	8	9	10
Very Weak				Average					Very Strong

Rating

1. Introduced a variety of topics   _____

2. Offered extra information when responding to questions   _____

3. Asked a number of questions   _____

4. Balanced speaking and listening   _____

5. Used conversational directors   _____

6. Avoided interrupting   _____

7. Added comments related to partner's comments   _____

8. Was polite   _____

9. Was ethical   _____

10. Overall Rating of Conversational Effectiveness   _____

Exercise 6.4   Name _____

I Like Talking to You

Purpose: To increase your awareness of the role ethical dialogue plays in effective conversation.

Instructions:

A. Effective conversationalists engage in ethical dialogue. Ethical dialogue consists of the following aspects. Familiarize yourself with them.
   An ethical conversationalist . . .
   1. Is authentic: if in disagreement, says so.
   2. Is empathetic: is able to imagine from the other person's point of view.
   3. Is confirming: expresses nonpossessive warmth.
   4. Is supportive: communicates praise of worthwhile efforts.
   5. Demonstrates presentness: a willingness to listen actively.
   6. Treats conversational partners as equals.

B. Engage in a conversation with another person in class focusing on an issue on which you hold opposing views. Attempt to employ all six aspects of ethical dialogue.

C. Following the conversation, both partners complete the "ethical dialogue" evaluation form on the next page.

D. Discuss with your conversation partner the evaluation that you both completed. Explain what aspects of the conversation made you feel "good" about yourself based upon what your partner said or did.

Discussion:

ETHICAL DIALOGUE EVALUATION

Rate your conversation partner using the following scale:

1	2	3	4	5	6	7	8	9	10
Not				At					Frequently
At All				Times					

Rating

1. Authentic (stated disagreement)   _____
    Explain:

2. Empathetic (seemed to imagine from my view)   _____
    Explain:

3. Confirming (expressed nonpossessive warmth)   _____
    Explain:

4. Supportive (communicated praise of my efforts)   _____
    Explain:

5. Demonstrated presentness (willingness to actively listen)   _____
    Explain:

6. Treated me as an equal   _____
    Explain:

7. Overall Rating of Ethical Dialogue   _____

Exercise 6.5

Name _____

It Feels Good to Know Someone is Listening

Purpose: To enhance your ability to participate in an effective conversation by making sure that your comments relate to those previously made by others.

Instructions:

A. Enter a conversation with another person, making sure to give that person your full attention.

B. When it is your turn to speak, make sure that you relate what you say directly to what that person said, reassuring that person that you have been giving him/her your full attention. For example: "Muhammad, you said that you've been stressed lately. Is there anything that I could do to help?"

C. Complete this exercise with five different people.

D. Make note of the behavior of each person to whom you spoke. Does he/she appear to be complimented by your effort to pick up on what he/she said? Did your conversational behavior feel "different" than your normal conversational behavior? If so, how?

E. Discuss with the class how this exercise made you feel.

	Behavior Exhibited
Partner #1	
Partner #2	
Partner #3	
Partner #4	
Partner #5	

Exercise 6.6   Name _____

You're Disgusting and I Never Want to Talk to You Again

Purpose: To explore a partner's willingness to engage in ethical dialogue.

Instructions:
A. Fabricate an unethical position. For example: A plan to cheat on the next exam or plan to cheat on a partner.
B. Enter three separate conversations with individuals whom you know well. At some point in the conversation, share your "unethical" position. Ask your conversation partner whether or not he/she approves of your plan. (Following this conversation, carefully explain that you were completing an assignment for your class. Your friend may feel that you placed him/her in an unethical situation.)
C. Using the chart below, indicate with a + or – how effectively your conversation partners employed the following ethical dialogue strategies:
 1. Authentic: If in disagreement, says so.
 2. Empathetic: Imagined the situation from your point of view.
 3. Confirming: Expressed non-possessive warmth.
 4. Demonstrates presentness: Listened actively.
 5. Demonstrates equality: Treated you as an equal.
 6. Supportive: Communicated praise of worthwhile efforts.
D. Consider which of these partners you would most trust to tell his/her honest reaction.

ETHICAL DIALOGUE CHART

Use + to indicate effective use of strategy.
Use – to indicate ineffective use of strategy.

	Authentic	Empathetic	Confirming	Present	Equal	Supportive
Partner #1						
Partner #2						
Partner #3						

SELF EXAMINATION – CHAPTER 6

True/False If false, explain what is wrong with the statement.

___1. "I'm sorry for bothering you" is an example of positive politeness.

_____

___2. Saying "nothing" is one of the strategies one might consider when confronted with face threatening issues.

_____

___3. Accommodation is the courteous submission to the opinions, wishes, or judgment of another.

_____

___4. "Absolutely" is a word one might expect to hear from a low-context communicator.

_____

___5. The "quality" maxim for successful conversations calls for information that is on topic.

_____

Multiple Choice

___6. Which of the following is NOT a conversation rule?
  A. Rules must be followed.
  B. Rules are prescriptive.
  C. Rules may or may not be applicable.
  D. Rules specify appropriate human behavior.

___7. A pragmatic problem-consideration conversation begins with which step?
  A. One person initiates a topic requiring deliberation.
  B. Partners exchange and process information.
  C. Partners clarify steps for the conversation.
  D. Partners greet each other and engage in small talk.

___8. Effective conversationalists recognize and heed turn-exchanging cues. Which of the following is LEAST likely to be interpreted as a turn-exchanging cue?
  A. pause
  B. lowered volume
  C. a question
  D. raised head

___9. Which of the following lines is LEAST likely to be spoken by a high-context communicator?

A.   "Luc, I'm positive that you are right."

B.   "Luc, I agree."

C.   "Luc (silence)."

D.   "Luc, I'll have to think about what you said." (frown)

___10. Successful conversations observe six maxims. Which of the following is NOT one of the maxims?

A.   give truthful information

B.   give enough but not TOO much information

C.   be ethical

D.   ask questions

Complete the Thought

11.   Statements that respect the desire of the other to be appreciated and approved are referred to by Brown and Levinson as expressions of _____.

12.   Successful conversations observe maxims. The maxim calling for specific, organized communication of thought is known as the _____.

Essay Questions

13.   Verderber and Verderber highlight five components of ethical dialogue. Explain them.

14.   Low-context communicators and high-context communicators may run into serious communication problems. Explain.

Interpersonal Problem Solver

You're home for Spring Break. Things haven't gone well this semester and your grades are much lower than expected. So far, you've managed to avoid a discussion of grades with your parents and you're headed back to school tomorrow. Unfortunately, your luck has run out. At the dinner table with siblings, parents, and grandparents, your grandma asks, "So, honey, how are your grades this semester?" Based upon your understanding of the maxims for successful conversation, how do you respond and why?

Chapter 7: Listening Effectively

Interactive Chapter Outline

I.   Listening—the process of receiving, constructing meaning from, and responding to spoken and/or nonverbal messages—requires distinct, specific skills.

    A.   Listening is a fundamental skill that affects the quality of our conversations.

    B.   Listening shapes the course of our relationships. In a recent phone conversation with a friend, I spent several minutes explaining my plans for the weekend. He then spent several minutes sharing his weekend plans. When he was done, he said, "So what are your plans for the weekend?" Ouch! How would you rate yourself as a listener? Can you identify an instance when poor listening affected your relationship?

    _____

    _____

    C.   Listening is underrated as a communication skill. After 48 hours many listeners remember about 25% of what they heard. Think about the last exam you took in one of your courses. If you had to take that same exam today, do you think you would remember the material? Why?

    _____

II. Attending, the perceptual process of selecting specific stimuli from the countless stimuli that reach the senses, is the first phase of the listening process.

    A.   Good listeners exercise psychological control over sounds we choose to attend to. When you listen to someone, are you able to tune out other sounds? When you were in elementary school and high school, did you study with the radio blaring? TV on? Lots of noise in the background? Were you able to tune out the sounds?

    _____

    B.   Poor listeners exercise insufficient control over which sounds they attend to. Do you "need" an absolutely quiet room to study in? Why/Why not?

    _____

III. Four techniques help us to consciously focus our attention.

    A.   Get physically and mentally ready to listen. Verderber and Verderber suggest that you should sit up, lean forward, and avoid physical movement. Are these ways that you employ to get "physically ready?" Explain. When you are sitting in a lecture hall, do you block out miscellaneous thoughts? How? Do you often find yourself "off" on another topic? Which classes? Why?

_____

_____

B.   Make the shift from speaker to listener complete. Don't plan your next words while the other person is speaking. When you meet someone new, are you so uncomfortable that you miss everything he/she is saying because you are planning your next words? Why do you think you do that?

_____

_____

C.   Hear a person out before you react.
1.   Don't let mannerisms and words interfere with hearing. I'm annoyed by "um, ah" and body scratching. What annoys you? What do you do to stop these mannerisms and words from interfering?

_____

_____

2.   Don't tune out irritating ideas. I dislike "pro-death-penalty" positions and "anti-welfare" positions and "how-to-get-rich" conversations. What positions irritate you? How do you stop yourself from tuning out?

_____

_____

3.   Don't let semantic noise stop you from listening. The word *gal* pushes my semantic noise button. What words push your button? How do you address this semantic noise?

_____

_____

D.   Adjust the listening behavior to the situation. Listening for pleasure requires less attending than listening for learning. Critical listening requires serious attending.

IV.   Active listening involves four procedures.

A.   Active listeners pay attention to and seek out organizational patterns. "What is her point? What proof does she offer?" Do you listen more actively in some of your classes than others? Which ones? Why?

_____

_____

B.   Active listeners attend to nonverbal cues. One of my students stopped me in the hallway to say that she had missed class because of her fiance's illness. She added that she might have to miss more classes. This student was normally vibrant. On that particular day, her face appeared drained of emotion. I placed my hand on her shoulder and said, "Kathy, I'm sorry about your fiance. How is he doing?" She started to cry as she said, "He's in a coma. He isn't expected to live."

C. Active listeners ask questions that observe the following four guidelines:
1.   Questions note the kind of information you need to increase your understanding.

After my son's death, colleagues would pass me in the hallway and say, "Hi, Mary, how's it going?" On bad days, I'd say, "Not well" or "I'm taking it by the minute." Or, on particularly gray days I'd respond, "I'm alive." It was amazing to me how many of my colleagues just kept on walking, as though they had heard the expected answer, "Fine." Once in awhile, a colleague would hear my words and tone, stop, turn around, put an arm on my shoulder and ask, "Is there something I can do to help, Mary?" When this happened, I knew that my colleague was actively listening. Have you had a similar listening experience where others failed to question? How did it make you feel?

_____

_____

2.   Questions are phrased as complete sentences. Some of my colleagues would respond with "Fine? Just fine?" The abruptness of their questions caused me to dismiss them with lines like "Oh, things could be worse, I guess."

3.   Questions are asked with carefully monitored nonverbal cues that convey genuine interest and concern.

My colleague Noreen has such care in her voice that I feel her support before words are ever spoken. She'll knock on my office door, step inside, sit down in the chair across from mine, look directly into my face, pause, and say, "How are things today?" Her nonverbal concern unleashes my grief and tears flood to the surface. Do you know someone whose nonverbal cues signal warmth? Can you identify those cues?

_____

_____

D. Active listeners paraphrase by putting their understanding of a message into words.
1.   Paraphrases focus on content, feelings underlying content, or both.
2.   The purpose of a paraphrase is to make sure that you really understand

what the speaker means by what he or she said.

Read the following and prepare a content paraphrase, a feelings paraphrase, then one that does both: "I'm so angry with my roommate. I can't deal with her anymore. She criticizes everything I say and do. I've had it. I want out." Content paraphrase: _____

_____

Feelings paraphrase: _____

_____

Content/Feelings paraphrase: _____

_____

3. Paraphrases should be used for five specific purposes:
   a. Listener needs better understanding of message
   b. Misunderstanding will have serious consequences
   c. Message is long and contains complex ideas
   d. Emotional strain was present
   e. English is not the speaker's native language

V. Active listeners use skills to help increase retention of information.

A. Repeat information. If not repeated, short-term memory may hold it for as little as 20 seconds. Repeat names/directions immediately and repeatedly. "His name is Moua Vang, Moua Vang, Moua Vang, Moua Vang." How often do you forget someone's name immediately after you have been told?

_____

B. Construct mnemonics (artificial techniques used as memory aids). What mnemonic would you create to help you remember the following grocery items: toothbrush, toothpaste, hamburger, onions, and olives? What saying would you create to help you remember the name "Professor Ferrari?"

_____

C. Take notes. Writing out ideas requires you to take a more active role in the listening process. Do you find that you do better in classes where you take notes?

D. Evaluate.
   1. Analyze what you have understood.
   2. Interpret it in order to determine how truthful, authentic, or believable you judge the meaning to be. Have you failed to listen critically and wound up supporting an idea that violated your own values?

VI.   Critical listening requires work.

     A.   Separate facts from inferences.
         1.   A fact is a statement whose accuracy can be verified. "Jamal is a doctor."
         2.   An inference is a claim or assertion based on observation or fact. "Jamal studied hard to become a doctor."

     B.   Analyze the facts to determine their truth.
         1.   Question whether the stated or implied relevance between the facts and the inference makes sense.
         2.   Question whether there is any other known information that lessens the quality of the inference.

Judge the validity of the following inference using the facts provided.
Inference #1: The professor who teaches this course treats students fairly.

Facts:
a.   She allows students to retake failed exams.
b.   She allows two absences without a grade drop.
c.   She failed Latisha, but Latisha missed four classes.

Use the following questions to evaluate the inference:
(1)   Is there meaningful factual information to support it? How meaningful are the factual statements concerning a retake policy and an absentee policy to one's determination of fairness?
(2)   Is the factual support true? Is the factual support relevant to the inference? Can you demonstrate what sense it makes that a fair teacher is someone who allows retake exams and absences?
(3)   Is there known information which would prevent the inference from logically following the factual statement? Does the fact that the professor failed someone for missing 4 classes lessen the quality of the inference?

_____

_____

_____

_____

_____

VII.   *Inter-Action Dialogue:* Good listening requires specific behavior.

     A.   Attending

B.   Understanding through the use of questions and paraphrase

C.   Remembers through repetition and the use of mnemonics

D.   Analyzing by evaluating inferences.

View the Inter-Action CD and refer to the script of this conversation in your text in order to analyze Jill's listening behavior. Which specific listening behavior appears to be Jill's strongest? Did Jill sound sincere to you, or did she sound as though she were "practicing" good listening behavior? If you were Gloria, would you feel good about having run into Jill? When you have a problem, is Jill a person to whom you would go if you were seeking a good listener? Explain.

_____

_____

_____

_____

_____

_____

Key Terms in Chapter 7
(Define each of the terms below.)

active listening _____

_____

attending _____

_____

critical listening _____

_____

evaluating _____

_____

factual statement _____

_____

inference _____

_____

listening _____

_____

mnemonic device _____

_____

paraphrase _____

_____

Interesting Sites on the Internet

http://www.drnadig.com/listening.htm

    Larry Nadig, clinical psychologist and marriage and family therapist, offers tips on effective listening.

http://bbll.com/ch02.html

    This site introduces you to entrepreneur and author Bryan Bell's work on barriers to interpersonal listening in his book, *Lessons in Lifemanship*.

http://www.coping.org/communi/listen.htm

    James M. Messina, Ph.D. and Constance M. Messina, Ph.D. offer suggestions for improving listening skills and include a listening role-playing activity.

http://www.vandruff.com/art_converse.html

    Authors Dean and Marshall VanDruff identify and explain various acts of conversational cheap shots in the hope that we will recognize and avoid the acts.

http://www.bly.com/Pages/documents/CEPARTLISTEN1.htm

    In this site, Robert Bly, director of the Center for Technical Communication, presents the four steps of listening and six tips to guide one in becoming a better listener.

Exercise 7.1   Name _____

Why Don't You Listen to Me?

Purpose: To create an awareness of steps a listener can take to improve listening.

Instructions:
A. We all have them, friends whom, for whatever reason, we tend to "tune out." You know, the friend who says, "You never listen to me!" Choose one of those friends. (Hopefully, your list isn't too long)
B. Review the following five steps which help focus attention:
   1. Eliminate physical impediments to listening: TV, loud music, etc.
   2. Get physically and mentally ready to listen. (Sit up, lean forward, and focus eyes and mind on your friend.)
   3. Refrain from planning your next words until your friend has finished speaking. Keep listening.
   4. Hear the person out before you react. (Don't get caught up in semantic noise or start tuning out irritating ideas. Don't focus on annoying mannerisms.)
   5. Adjust to the listening goals (are you listening for pleasure? learning?).
C. Have the conversation.
D. In the space below, evaluate the results of this exercise. Were the five steps useful? Did your friend notice that you were "attending" better than usual? Did you feel better about your attending behavior?

_____

Evaluation:

Exercise 7.2

Name _____

Look at Me When I'm Talking to You!

Purpose: To increase awareness of poor attending behaviors that serve as an impediment to listening.

Instructions:

A. Go to the student union and observe three different pairs of speakers for 5 minutes each. Sit close enough to eavesdrop.

B. Use the following check list to evaluate their "attending" behavior. In the appropriate space, make a check each time you observe the behavior.

C. Discuss the results of your survey with students in class. How well do students appear to attend based upon the results of your mini-survey?

ATTENDING SURVEY

ATTENDING BEHAVIORS	Listener 1A	Listener 1B	Listener 2A	Listener 2B	Listener 3A	Listener 3B
1. Sat up straight						
2. Slouched						
3. Leaned toward speaking partner						
4. Leaned away from speaking partner						
5. Focused eyes on partner						
6. Focused eyes away from partner						
7. Nodded head affirmingly						
8. Asked questions						

Exercise 7.3   Name_____

Friend, Can You Spare a Minute?

Purpose: To determine how well your friends actively and critically listen to what you say.

Instructions:

A. Identify 2 students on campus whom you consider to be good friends.
B. Identify a problem you are "really" having. Don't invent one! Make an inference and support it with facts. For example: "I'm afraid I'm going to fail calculus. The instructor has something against me." Or "I'm afraid my relationship with _____ is ending. She/he doesn't speak to me anymore."
C. Ask your friends for advice.
D. Complete the following listening evaluation.
E. React to the critical listening behavior of your friends. Was it clear that they were listening critically? Did their listening behavior prove helpful?

CRITICAL LISTENING EVALUATION

LISTENER . . .	FRIEND #1		FRIEND #2	
	YES	NO	YES	NO
1. was physically attentive?				
2. attended to my nonverbal cues?				
3. repeated things I said?				
4. paraphrased what I said?				
5. analyzed what I said?				
6. asked information-gathering questions?				
7. questioned the interpretation of events?				
8. questioned the accuracy of facts?				
9. questioned relationship of relevant facts and the inference?				

Exercise 7.4   Name _____

I'm Sorry, I Forgot Your Name

Purpose:
1. To create an awareness of our own poor attending behaviors.
2. To improve our attending behaviors.

Instructions:
PART ONE
    A. Identify 5 students in your classes whose first names you don't know.
    B. Ask each student his/her name.
    C. The next time you see the student, see if you can recall his/her name.
PART TWO
    D. Identify 5 more students in your classes whose first names you don't know.
    E. Ask each student his/her name.
    F. Repeat the name five times to yourself immediately after hearing it.
    G. The next time you see the student, see if you can recall his/her name.

Discuss with students in class whether or not name repetition helped you to remember names. If not, why not? What other tricks do students use for remembering names?

DISCUSSION:

Exercise 7.5   Name _____

I'm Sorry, Were You Saying Something?

Purpose: To increase awareness of physical and mental impediments to effective listening.

Instructions:
A. Review the following techniques for effective listening:
   1. Select specific stimuli to which you will attend, tuning out all other sounds.
   2. Get physically ready to listen by sitting up, leaning forward, and avoiding movement.
   3. Get mentally ready to listen by blocking out miscellaneous thoughts.
   4. Avoid planning your next words.
   5. Avoid reacting until you have heard the person out.
B. Engage in three separate conversations, making sure that you attend to each of the effective listening techniques.
C. Use the chart below to evaluate how well you employed the effective listening techniques.
D. Come to class prepared to discuss which of the effective listening techniques you found most difficult to employ. Which of the techniques was the easiest to use? Did conscious use of these techniques improve your listening? How so?

---

	1 = poor 2 = average 3 = good				
	Tunes Out Stimuli	**Physical Prep**	**Mental Prep**	**Avoids Planning**	**Avoids Reacting**
Partner #1					
Partner #2					
Partner #3					

Exercise 7.6   Name _____

When I Talk, I Know She's Listening

Purpose:
1. To become more familiar with the listening habits of successful people.
2. To test the hypothesis that successful people are where they are because they are good listeners.

Instructions:
A. Identify 3 people whom you believe to be successful (an ambiguous word, I know.)
B. Engage in conversations with each of these 3 individuals.
C. Rate their listening in the seven categories listed in the table below.
D. Discuss with a partner whether or not you find these characteristics to be valuable indicators of good listening and whether you associate these characteristics with successful people.

LISTENING CATEGORIES	PERSON #1	PERSON #2	PERSON #3
1. Pays attention?			
2. Is courteous?			
3. Nods head?			
4. Repeats the statement?			
5. Avoids being judgmental?			
6. Asks follow-up questions?			
7. Listens with entire body?			

SELF EXAMINATION - CHAPTER 7

True/False If false, explain what is wrong with the statement.

___1. Active listeners try to tune out nonverbal cues.

_____

___2. Sitting up and leaning forward are techniques that focus attention.

_____

___3. *Sweetie Pie, babe,* and *boy* are words that may interfere with listening. If so, the words are referred to as semantic noise.

_____

___4. A "focused" listener hears the person out before reacting.

_____

___5. Active listeners refrain from asking questions until the speakers have finished.

_____

Multiple Choice

___6. Active listening involves four procedures. Identify those four procedures.
   A.   Seek out organizational patterns/attend to nonverbal cues/ask questions/ paraphrase.
   B.   Seek out organizational patterns/tune out irritating ideas/attend to nonverbal cues/paraphrase
   C.   Seek out organizational patterns/attend to nonverbal cues/ask questions/tune out semantic noise
   D.   Attend to nonverbal cues/ask questions/paraphrase/tune out irritating ideas

___7. Which of the following is an inference?
   A.   My mother worked 40 hours last week.
   B.   Leandre studied until midnight last night.
   C.   Austin's parents were married in June 19, 1971.
   D.   Sehaya worked hard to finish third in the race last Saturday.

___8. Verderber and Verderber cite four techniques that help listeners to consciously focus attention. Which of the following is NOT one of the four recommended techniques?
   A.   Eliminate physical impediments to listening.
   B.   Relax physically and mentally.
   C.   Don't plan your next words when the other person is speaking.
   D.   Hear a person out before you react.

___9. A critical listener evaluates inferences. Identify which of the following is the most valid inference.
- A. Kelly is an excellent student. She spends 5 hours every evening doing homework.
- B. Pete is a poor student. He received two F's last semester.
- C. Ariane's career in marketing is rewarding. Every week she travels to a different city in the United States.
- D. Ahmad's education was costly. He spent $100,000 in tuition for the four years it took to earn his B.A. degree.

___10. After 48 hours a listener typically remembers what percentage of a conversation?
- A. 10%
- B. 25%
- C. 40%
- D. 50%

Complete the Thought

11. I have four things to buy at the store: deodorant, pens, envelopes and Oil of Olay moisturizing cream. I don't have a pencil or paper so I mentally create the word "DOPE" to help me remember. This is an example of a(n) _____.

12. The perceptual process of selecting specific stimuli from the countless stimuli that reach the senses is known as _____.

Essay Questions

13. Critical listening requires a listener to evaluate an inference based upon the following:
    - a. the amount of meaningful factual information to support it.
    - b. the relevance of the factual supports.
    - c. known information which would prevent the inference from logically following the factual statements.

    Use these three steps to evaluate the following inference:

    Ling Lee is brilliant. She has a 4.0 gradepoint. She was accepted at both Harvard and Yale. She received a 40 on her ACT.

14. "I'm failing English Lit. I just can't pay attention to Professor Hasman. He wears the same shirt to class every day. He's got chalk all over himself by the end of the lecture. The guy is brilliant. He knows what he's talking about. I really want to learn. I sit back in my seat and try to listen, but my mind keeps wandering." What advice can you offer this student?

Interpersonal Problem Solver

The semester has just begun and you have a new roommate. The phone rings and your roommate answers. You can hear that the caller has disturbing news. From what you can make out, someone may have died. Your roommate hangs up, goes over to his/her bed and lies down. Applying what you have learned about active listening, what might you say and do?

Chapter 8: Responding with Understanding and Comforting Others

Interactive Chapter Outline

I.   Responses to a partner's emotional distress can affect the partner's ability to cope as well as affect the relationship.

      A.   An escape strategy dismisses the importance of a partner's problem.

            For example, a friend recently asked me how my Christmas was. I told her that I had the flu on Christmas Eve and Christmas Day but that I was happy to stay in bed because it seemed better than the alternative, finding something to be happy about (my son Ryan, a police officer, had recently been found dead in his squad car). My friend paused and then told me about the delicious ham that she had fixed for Christmas dinner. Have you ever shared a distressful experience with a friend, only to be dismissed? How did it make you feel? What effect did it have on your relationship with that person?

            _____

            _____

            _____

            _____

      B.   Comforting responses provide solace and help to solve problems.

            When my daughter told me how sorry she was that I had been sick on Christmas Day, I said, "Kelly, it wasn't so bad." She needed no explanation and said, "I know, Mom, I miss Ryan, too." Her words told me that I wasn't alone. Have you experienced the comforting solace of a friend or loved one? How did it make you feel? What effect did it have on your relationship with that person?

            _____

            _____

            _____

            _____

II.   Appropriate supportive responses depend on our ability to empathize with our communication partner.

      A.   Empathy is the cognitive process of identifying with or vicariously experiencing the feelings, thoughts, or attitudes of another. It was obvious that Kelly was vicariously experiencing my pain, a pain that she, too, felt intensely.

B.   Empathy is a process that requires more effort with someone who is very different or who is experiencing something out of our realm of experience.

One of my students came to my office to tell me that he is gay and that his AIDS-infected partner was dying. I have never experienced society's discrimination against my sexual orientation, nor have I experienced its lack of compassion toward any illness that I contracted. A long pause preceded my comforting words, a pause filled with fear that I wouldn't find the right words to ease his pain. Have you experienced a similar situation? Were you able to find the right words?

III.   Scholars have identified three different approaches that people can use when empathizing.

A.   Empathic responsiveness is experiencing an emotional response parallel to another person's actual or anticipated display of emotion. A close or intimate relationship with the other person allows you to experience the response along with the other. Kelly's closeness to me, and to her brother Ryan, facilitated her empathic response.

B.   Perspective taking is imagining yourself in the place of another. We assume how we would feel and assume that the other person feels the same.

Police just caught my friend's son rolling a joint in a men's bathroom. He was arrested and released. My friend was devastated. I tried to imagine how I would have felt if my son or daughter had been arrested for doing something similar. Interestingly enough, I wasn't able to feel my friend's pain. Instead, I found myself thinking that her son had just had a terrific learning experience. Have you had a similar experience with a friend where you were unable to imagine yourself in his/her place? How did you respond?

_____

_____

_____

C.   Sympathetic responsiveness is your feeling of concern, compassion, or sorrow for another because of the situation.
1.   You don't attempt to experience the feelings of the other.
2.   You intellectually understand what the speaker has said and experience concern, compassion, or sorrow for that person.

I did feel concern for my friend whose son had been briefly incarcerated. I was sorry for her pain. Have you experienced a similar sympathetic response?

IV.   Interpersonal effectiveness can be increased by improving our ability to empathize.

    A.   Take the time to understand the person who is speaking by paying serious attention to what he/she says and feels. What do you hear Linda Howard (Diverse Voices) saying as she talks about her mixed identity?

_____

_____

_____

    B.   Treat the person as a person with value and not an object. How does this advice apply to Linda's co-worker Nellie? How did Linda apply this advice in her treatment of Nellie (Diverse Voices)?

_____

_____

_____

_____

_____

    C.   Effective empathetic responses depend upon your ability to clearly read the nonverbal message sent out.
       1.   Primary emotions such as happiness, sadness, surprise, anger, and fear are recognized with greater than 90 percent accuracy.
       2.   Contempt, disgust, interest, determination, and bewilderment are recognized with 80 to 90 percent accuracy.

    D.   Two silently posed questions help to improve observational skills:
       1.   What emotions do I believe the person is experiencing right now?
       2.   What are the cues the person is giving that I am using to draw this conclusion?

Silently pose these questions as you observe a friend. Then, based upon your answers, take time to question your friend on your observations. Did you accurately read your friend?

Just last night, Sue and I were speaking to a friend. When the friend started to talk about her nephew, her mood changed. She furrowed her brow, squinted her eyes, and said, "I really hope he doesn't come to visit." Sue said, "I'm sensing that you are very upset with your nephew. What's wrong?" My friend started to cry and said that she had recently learned that her nephew had molested a child. She had kept this information to herself for weeks. Sue's observation and question allowed our friend an opportunity to share.

V.   Empathy is much more difficult across cultures.

    A.   Communication behaviors carry different meanings in different cultures.
        1.   If you are speaking to someone who was born in the U.S., you can be reasonably sure that a giggle indicates amusement.
        2.   If you are speaking to someone who recently emigrated from Japan, a giggle is more likely to convey discomfort. Have you experienced difficulty reading the communication behavior of someone from another culture? How did you address the problem?

_____

_____

_____

    B.   Indifference to strangers causes us to be less motivated to attend to nonverbal cues. Are there students from different cultures in your class to whom you have displayed such indifference?

    C.   Be more attentive than normal to the nonverbal behavior of people from different cultures.
        1.   Attend to their nonverbal cues.
        2.   If in doubt, take time to ask how the person is feeling.

Engage in a conversation with a student in one of your classes who is relatively new to the United States. Attend to his/her nonverbal cues. Ask questions based upon his/her cues. What did you notice?

_____

_____

_____

I've had Native American students in my Public Speaking class for years. I was aware that when I spoke to some Native American students, they directed their eyes away from me. While I attended to their nonverbal cues, it took me several semesters before I finally asked one of the students why she avoided direct eye contact with me. Aimee explained that she felt direct eye contact was disrespectful. Following that conversation, I became more empathetic to Aimee as she struggled to adhere to my requirement to use direct eye contact with the audience during speeches. I have since modified my requirement.

VI.   Many times, we will be called upon to comfort a speaker.

A.   To comfort means to help people feel better about themselves and their behavior. Describe a time you comforted someone. Explain why you felt your efforts were/were not successful.

_____

_____

_____

_____

_____

B.   Comforting occurs when one feels respected, understood, and confirmed. Describe a friend's successful effort to comfort you. What did he/she say and how did it make you feel?

_____

_____

_____

_____

_____

C.   Some comforting responses show approval of a person's feelings or acknowledge the person's right to have those feelings.

When my husband left me, after twenty-five years of marriage, I experienced a period of rage. My best friend Peggy would listen to my venomous rampages. She'd say, "Go ahead, Mary, let it out! You're a wonderful woman! You deserved to be treated better." Sometimes my gentle friend would even join in. When we were finished, we'd both laugh.

VII.   Comforting responses are efforts to commiserate.

A.   Comforting responses reassure, encourage, soothe, console, bolster, and cheer up.

B.   Comforting responses show we care.

C.   Comforting responses demonstrate that the listener empathizes with a person's feelings, whatever their direction or intensity.

D.   Effective supportive statements must be in touch with facts.

VIII.   Two supportive approaches provide comfort.

    A.   Comforting statements show empathy, sensitivity, and may show a willingness to be actively involved, if need be.

    B.   Supporting positive feelings requires that you appreciate how the other person feels and how you would feel under the same circumstance. Think of positive news that you recently shared with a friend. How did he/she respond? How did the response make you feel?

    _____

    _____

    _____

    _____

    C.   Supporting negative feelings requires that you support that person's feelings and support that person's right to those feelings.

    Following my son's death, his grandmother said, "Mary, without Ryan, there is nothing to live for." I wanted to say, "You have five beautiful grandchildren. Live for them!" But, I knew that the time wasn't right. Lois needed my support. I said, "Ryan adored you, Lois, as much as you adored him. I can't imagine life without Ryan either."

IX.   Comforting strategies are messages that have the goal of relieving or lessening the emotional distress of others.

    A.   Sophisticated messages acknowledge, elaborate, and legitimize the feelings of another person.

    B.   Sophisticated messages are:
        1.   Aimed at discovering how the distressed person feels.
        2.   Less evaluative.
        3.   Feeling centered.
        4.   More likely to accept the point of view of the other.
        5.   More likely to offer explanations for the feelings being expressed.

    My friend Pam knew that my son Ryan's birthday was approaching (Ryan had died eight months earlier). Pam invited me to spend Ryan's birthday at her home in Madison, Wisconsin, where my son had gone to college. On the phone, she carefully questioned me about how I wanted to celebrate. I told her that I just needed to find a way to make it through the day without being consumed with sadness. I also wanted to celebrate in a way that would make Ryan proud. When I arrived at Pam's home, she had a bouquet of helium-filled birthday balloons and a set of beer glasses from which we toasted my son. We dined at Ryan's favorite Mexican restaurant where Pam listened as I shared mother-son stories. She laughed and cried with me. Her sophisticated attention to my feelings allowed her to devise a celebration that Ryan would have loved. I could hear him saying, "Way to go, Mom!" Describe a time when someone effectively comforted you.

_____

_____

_____

_____

_____

X.   Comforting benefits the comforter. (Researcher Brant Burleson, Purdue University)

    A.   Effective comforting increases our own self-esteem.

    B.   Effective comforters are better liked by the one being comforted.

    C.   Effective comforters are better liked by those who see them effectively comfort others.

    D.   Effective comforters have better long-term relationships.

        I will never forget Pam for the comfort that she gave me on Ryan's birthday. Is there a person in your life who has brought you comfort? How has it affected your relationship?

_____

_____

_____

_____

XI.   Effective emotional support messages share common characteristics.

    A.   The goal of an effective support message is to create a conversational environment that encourages the person needing support to talk about and make sense of the situation that is causing distress.

    B.   According to Burleson, effective and helpful supportive messages do the following:
        1.   Clearly state that the speaker's aim is to help.

2. Express acceptance, love, and affection for the other.
3. Demonstrate care, concern, and interest in the other's situation.
4. Indicate availability to listen and support.
5. State that the speaker is an ally.
6. Acknowledge the others' feelings and situation and express sincere sympathy.
7. Assure the other that what they are feeling is legitimate.
8. Encourage the other to elaborate.

Think of a friend in need of emotional support. Then, using Burleson's findings concerning effective supportive messages, write a supportive message below. Share that message with a friend.

_____

_____

_____

_____

XII. Ineffective emotional support messages share common characteristics.

A. An ineffective support message fails to create a conversational environment that encourages the person needing support to talk about and make sense of the situation that is causing distress.

B. According to Burleson, ineffective and unhelpful supportive messages do the following:
1. Condemn and criticize the other's feelings and behavior.
2. Imply that the other's feelings are not warranted.
3. Tell the other how to feel about the situation or that they should ignore how they feel about the situation.
4. Focus attention on the speaker by a lengthy recount of a similar situation faced by the speaker.
5. Intrude because they represent a level of involvement or concern greater than appropriate for the relationship.

Recently, I gave ineffective emotional support by intruding at a level far too great for the type of relationship that a student and I shared. I had heard from another professor that one of my students had been raped. It was the beginning of the semester and I had more than a hundred students in my class. I barely knew the young woman. One afternoon, she walked by my office, looking upset. I stepped outside of my office and called out her name. I said, "I've noticed that you've been looking very sad recently. If you ever need someone to talk to, please know that I'm willing to listen." She stared at me for the longest time and then walked away. It wasn't until the end of the semester, after she had come to know and trust me, that she came to me for support. Have you ever given ineffective emotional support? Explain.

_____

_____

_____

_____

_____

XIII. Supportive interactions seem to progress through four well-ordered phases.

    A.   Support activation occurs.
        1.   Something happens to trigger a supportive response.
        2.   Support is activated either by the people needing comfort or by the comforter.

    B.   Support provision occurs.
        1.   Comforters enact messages to give support by focusing on the emotions being displayed, or;
        2.   Comforters enact messages to give support by focusing on the problem expressed.

    C.   Target reaction occurs.
        1.   The person being comforted reacts to the help.
        2.   He/she indicates how successful the helper's message was.

    D.   Helper responses occur.
        1.   If the person in need of comfort is more stable, the helper may respond by changing the focus of the conversation.
        2.   If still in need of comfort, the interaction cycle backs to a previous phase and continues until one partner changes the topic or halts the conversation.

Recently, a student stopped me in the hallway to tell me why she had missed class. Her fiancé had had an asthma attack and was in a coma at a nearby hospital (support activation). I embraced her and told her not to worry about class; I'd help her catch up on whatever she had missed (support provision). She started to cry, hugged me, and said that she knew I'd understand (target reaction). I told her that she could stop by my office anytime if she needed someone to listen (helper response). She thanked me and walked away. (Her fiancé died the following week.)

XIV. Burleson identifies five supportive message skills.

A. Clarifying supportive intentions is the process of indicating that we are trying to support.
   1. Clarification of intentions helps our partner to put down his/her guard.
   2. Clarification of intentions may help partner feel better.
   3. Clarification of intentions involves four steps:
      a. State intention to help.
      b. Remind partner of commitment to relationship.
      c. Indicate that help is sole motive.
      d. Phrase clarification in a way that reflects helpfulness.

B. Buffer face threats by using both positive and negative politeness skills.

   1. **Positive facework messages** protect the partner's need to be respected, liked, and valued by verbally affirming the person or the person's actions in the present difficulty.
      a. Describe positive feelings about what the other said or did.
      b. Express admiration for the person's courage or effort.
      c. Acknowledge the difficulty of the situation.
      d. Express belief that the other has what it takes to endure.

   2. **Negative facework messages** support the partner's need for independence and autonomy by verbally using indirect methods when offering information, opinions, or advice.
      a. Form messages that ask for permission before making suggestions or giving advice.
      b. Verbally defer to opinions/preferences of other.
      c. Use tentative language to hedge and qualify opinions/advice.
      d. Offer suggestions indirectly through stories or hypothetical options.

   3. **Other-centered messages** involve the utilization of active listening, expression of compassion and understanding, encouragement of partner to talk and elaborate on what happened, and exploration of partner's feelings about what happened.
      a. Ask questions that prompt other to elaborate on what happened.
      b. Emphasize your willingness to listen regardless of time.
      c. Use vocalized encouragement and nonverbal behavior.
      d. Affirm, legitimize, and encourage exploration of partner's feelings.
      e. Demonstrate your understanding and connection with what happened while avoiding a change of focus to self.

4. **Framing** is the skill of providing comfort by offering information, observations, and opinions that enable receiver to better understand situation.
    a. Listen to how partner interprets events.
    b. Notice information partner may have overlooked or overemphasized.
    c. Clearly present relevant, truthful information that allows partner to reframe what happened.

5. **Advice giving messages** present relevant suggestions and proposals that a person could use to satisfactorily resolve a situation (generally expressed after preceding approaches have occurred).
    a. Ask for permission to advise.
    b. Word message as one of many possible suggestions.
    c. Present potential risks.
    d. Indicate no personal offense if advice is ignored.

My close friend Connie, a family therapist, knew that I was experiencing tremendous grief after the death of my son. The following is a conversation that she had with me: "Mary, you know how much I care about you (clarification). I'm amazed at how well you're coping with Ryan's death (positive facework). No one knows better than you what you need to do to get through this (negative facework). But, I was wondering if you had given any thought to therapy (other-centered)?" I explained that I was very sad and cried often, but that I thought that tears were a natural expression of any parent's grief. Connie nodded, looked directly into my eyes (other-centered), and said, "Mary, your crying might be a sign of depression (framing). If you don't want my advice, I'll understand. But I think therapy might be something you should consider (advice)."

Identify a friend who is experiencing a problem. Use each of Burleson's five supportive message skills to shape a supportive message for your friend. Write it below. Convey the message to your friend.

_____

_____

_____

_____

_____

_____

XV.   Gender and cultural similarities exist in comforting.

    A.   Men and women place a high value on emotional support from their partners.

    B.   Men and women have similar ideas about messages that do better and worse at reducing emotional distress.

    C.   Men and women find that messages which encourage exploration and elaboration of feelings provide the most comfort, although men are less likely to use other-centered messages.

    D.   Members of all social groups find that solace strategies, especially other-centered messages, provide the most support.

        Create a list of friends and relatives who have provided you with emotional support. Do you find that there are as many men on your list as there are women?

        _____

        _____

XVI.   Cultural differences exist in comforting.

    A.   European Americans, more than other American ethnic groups, believe open discussion of feelings helps the other person feel better.

    B.   Americans are more sensitive to other-centered messages than are Chinese.

    C.   Both Chinese and Americans, to an even greater extent, view avoidance strategies less appropriate than approach strategies.

    D.   Both married Chinese and married Americans view a spouse's emotional support to be the most important type of emotional support received.

    E.   African Americans (especially women) place lower value on partner emotional support skills than do European or Asian Americans.

        Ask friends and relatives who are divorced about the role that emotional support may have played in the breakup of the marriage. Discuss results below.

        _____

        _____

        _____

_____

_____

XVII. **_Inter-Action Dialogue:_** Providing emotional support requires specific behavior.

    A.   Empathizing

    B.   Clarifying supportive intentions

    C.   Positive and negative face work

    D.   Use of other-centered messages

    E.   Framing

    F.   Advice giving

View your Inter-Action CD ROM and read the script in your text to analyze Rob's comforting behavior. What do you think of the emotional support provided by Rob? Which specific behavior would you rate as Rob's strongest? Explain.

_____

_____

_____

_____

_____

_____

Do you think that Rob went "beyond" emotional support when he advised James to "let it go" or do you feel that his advice was appropriate? Is Rob the type of friend to whom you would turn if you were in need of emotional support? Explain.

_____

_____

_____

_____

_____

_____

Key Terms in Chapter 8
(Define each of the terms below.)

advice giving _____

_____

comfort _____

_____

empathic responsiveness _____

_____

empathy _____

_____

escape strategy _____

_____

framing _____

_____

negative facework _____

_____

other-centered messages _____

_____

perspective taking _____

_____

positive facework _____

_____

supporting positive feelings _____

_____

supporting responses _____

_____

supportive intentions _____

_____

supportive messages _____

_____

sympathetic responsiveness _____

_____

Interesting Sites on the Internet

http://mentalhelp.net/psyhelp/chap13/chap13d.htm

> Sponsored by Mental Health Net, this site offers suggestions for practicing empathic responses. The material is from Clayton Tucker-Ladd's book, *Psychological Self-Help*.

http://www.touch-another-heart.com/ch1.htm

> Dr. Lawrence J. Bookbinder, a psychotherapeutic counselor, describes how empathy and listening skills can lead to good relationships and emotional intimacy.

http://www.touch-another-heart.com/ch2.htm

> Dr. Lawrence J. Bookbinder discusses the psychological hug as an important benefit affecting the emotional intimacy of two people.

http://www.apa.org/pubinfo/altruism.html

> This site, sponsored by the American Psychological Association, discusses what makes kids care and gives suggestions on how to teach gentleness in a violent world.

http://quiz.ivillage.com/health/tests/eqtest2.htm

> This site examines your emotional quotient, EQ, and presents a questionnaire that hints at your EQ.

Exercise 8.1   Name _____

Wow! I Can't Imagine!

Purpose: To enhance your ability to imagine yourself in the place of another.

Instructions:
A. Select one of the comments listed below. Assume that it has been spoken to you by a
    student in this class with whom you have worked closely on several projects. A friendship
    is developing.
B. Write out a "perspective taking" response which expresses your ability to imagine yourself
    in the place of the other person.
C. With another student from class, role play the scenario you chose.
D. Discuss with your partner the effectiveness of your "perspective taking" response.

_____

1. "My mom called last night. She's leaving my dad. I just can't believe it. I thought
    they were happy."
2. "My boyfriend dumped me last week and today I found out I'm pregnant."
3. "I won't be back next semester. I'm out of money."
4. "You know I've been going through a lot of tests lately. Well, they think it's leukemia.
    But hey, everyone's got their problems, right?"

Scenario Chosen:

Perspective Taking Response:

Exercise 8.2   Name _____

Have I Got a Question for You!

Purpose:
1. To enhance your ability to ask effective questions which encourage another to speak.
2. To enhance your ability to ask effective questions which clarify information.
3. To enhance your ability to ask effective questions which elicit further information.

Instructions:
A. Choose a partner. Decide who is Partner A and who is Partner B.
B. In Scenario 1, Partner A asks questions that encourage Partner B to speak.
C. In Scenario 2, Partner B asks questions which attempt to clarify information offered by Partner A.
D. In Scenario 3, Partner B asks questions which attempt to elicit further information from Partner A.

Scenario 1:   Having A Bad Day
Partner A: "Hey, what's wrong? You really look bummed?"
Partner B: "I really don't feel like talking right now."
Partner A: ?????

Scenario 2:   Roommate Problems
Partner A: "Having you as a roommate drives me nuts."
Partner B: ?????

Scenario 3:   Vacation Plans
Partner A: "You want to join me and my friends over Break?"
Partner B: ?????

Exercise 8.3

Name _____

What Did You Just Say?

Purpose:
1. To enhance your ability to paraphrase the denotative meaning of a message.
2. To enhance your ability to paraphrase the emotions behind the words.

Instructions:
A. With a partner, take turns paraphrasing the following statements with content paraphrases that focus on the denotative meaning of the message.
B. With your partner, take turns paraphrasing the same statements with feelings paraphrases, focusing on the emotions behind the words.

#1. "I'll never take another course from him. I don't care if I do need one of his classes to complete my major. The guy is a jerk! He wouldn't even give me a chance to explain why I missed class last week. He said I might as well drop now because I didn't have a chance of passing. He could care less what's going on in my life!"

#2. "I don't know what to do. The doctor said I need to slow down. She thinks I'm headed for a breakdown. How am I supposed to slow down? I've got 18 credits this semester. Does she think I can afford to withdraw? It's too late to get my money back. Besides, withdrawing would stress me out even more than I am now."

Content Paraphrase #1

Content Paraphrase #2

Feelings Paraphrase #1

Feelings Paraphrase #2

Exercise 8.4   Name _____

Maybe He Doesn't Like You

Purpose: To enhance your ability to reframe information or experiences by offering a reasonable alternative explanation.

Instructions:
A. Read the following statements.
B. Write a plausible interpreting response for each comment which helps the individual understand the situation from a different perspective.

_____

1.   "My parents told me I couldn't go to Mexico with my roommates over Break. They don't trust me."

2.   "I never had a curfew when I was in high school. My parents could care less what time I made it home."

3.   "Our instructor never gives essay exams. He's too lazy to spend the time grading them."

4.   "I can't believe this university requires freshmen to live in the dorms. They're just after our money."

5.   "My parents are making me pay my own tuition. They've got plenty of money. They're just too selfish."

6.   "I called Erich twice last night and left a message with his roommate. He never called back. I don't think he's interested in me."

7.   "My boss wouldn't let me off yesterday. She just can't stand the thought of someone having fun while she's working."

8.   "I've sent three e-mails to my math professor asking her for help. She hasn't answered one of them. The jerk!"

Exercise 8.5   Name _____

Can I Help Remove the Wax in Your Ears?

Purpose: To convey to listeners the link between tangential responses and self-worth.

Instructions:

A. Prepare a series of tangential responses that digress from the focus of the current topic of discussion. For example, if the initial speaker is talking about an exam that he needs to study for that evening, respond with: "I'm going to the movie tonight. Do you want to join me?" If the speaker tells you about the vacation she is planning, respond with a comment about a class you are taking.

B. Engage in six separate conversations. Insert as many tangential responses as possible.

C. At the end of the conversation, explain to the initial speaker what your assignment was. Ask how the tangential responses made him/her feel.

D. With a partner, discuss how tangential responses make you feel and how you might best deal with friends who are guilty of making such responses.

E. Below, make a list of 5 "kind yet assertive" statements that you could use to alert the initial speaker to the fact that he/she didn't appear to be listening.

	Lines to Alert Tangential Speakers
1	
2	
3	
4	
5	

Exercise 8.6   Name _____

Would You Please Let Me Finish!

Purpose: To enhance your awareness of the negative toll that interrupting responses have on one's self-worth.

Instructions:

A. Engage in five 10-minute conversations with people of varying degrees of social status.
B. Count how many times each person interrupts you.
C. At the end of your conversation, tell the speaker how many times he/she interrupted you and ask if he/she was aware of interrupting.
D. Record the response of each person.
E. With a partner, discuss the possible link between social status and the number of interruptions. What social variable seemed to play a role in determining who was most/least likely to interrupt?

SPEAKER	NUMBER OF INTERRUPTS	EXPLANATION	SOCIAL STATUS
#1			
#2			
#3			
#4			
#5			

SELF-EXAMINATION – CHAPTER 8

True/False   If false, explain what is wrong with the statement.

___ 1. A speaker's sex is the main variable in determining who interrupts more.

_____

___ 2. A paraphrase that focuses on the emotions behind the words is a content paraphrase.

_____

___ 3. Empathy is the process of identifying with the feelings, thoughts, or attitudes of another.

_____

___ 4. An incongruous response is a digression from the focus of the current topic.

_____

___ 5. Empathic responses can be nurtured by extensive reading of literature.

_____

Multiple Choice

___ 6. Ranee and Vashones are quizzing each other for tomorrow's math exam. In response to Ranee's question, Vashone responds, "Ranee, I like the perfume you're wearing." He has used which of the following responses?
   A. incongruous
   B. interrupting
   C. tangential
   D. irrelevant

___ 7. Which of the following, although crucial, is NOT identified as one of the four steps to becoming a more effective empathizer?
   A. Actively attend to speaker's words.
   B. Paraphrase what the speaker said.
   C. Concentrate on both verbal and nonverbal messages.
   D. Attempt to determine speaker's emotional state by using behavioral cues.

___ 8. When Jordan's sister died, his friend Brogan experienced an emotional response parallel to Jordan's. Name that response.
   A. perspective taking
   B. sympathetic responsiveness
   C. empathic responsiveness
   D. tangential response

___ 9. Which of the following statements is NOT confirmed by studies mentioned in this chapter on the different ways that men and women perform in comforting response behavior?

    A.   Men lack the competence to perform comforting behaviors as sensitively and effectively as women.

    B.   Both men and women prefer highly person-centered comforting strategies.

    C.   Men and women agree that men are likely to use low levels of person-centered responses.

    D.   Women were perceived to be somewhat better than men in providing achievement-related support.

___ 10. Which of the following is NOT true of a sophisticated comforting message?

    A.   evaluative

    B.   listener-centered

    C.   accepting of the point of view of the other person

    D.   explains feelings expressed by the other

Complete the Thought

11.   Scholars have identified three different forms of empathy. Imagining ourselves in the place of another is known as _____ .

12.   When we experience an emotional response that parallels the actual or anticipated emotion of the other, this form of empathy is known as

_____ .

Essay Questions

13.   Verderber and Verderber believe that empathizing skills can be nurtured. Please explain and develop this four-step process.

14.   Your roommate's mother just called to tell your roommate that she has cancer. Describe the conversation that you might have with your roommate, applying what you know about the four phases of supportive interactions.

Interpersonal Problem Solver

In a phone conversation that you overheard, you learn that your roommate's mother has breast cancer. Your roommate's need for autonomy and independence causes you to hesitate before offering support. Applying what you have learned about negative politeness skills, prepare a message of comfort.

Chapter 9:   Sharing Personal Information: Self-Disclosure and Feedback

Interactive Chapter Outline

I.   Effective interpersonal communication requires some degree of self-disclosure.

    A.   The Social Penetration Theory says that relational partners go back and forth between achieving more intimacy by disclosing more and developing distance by refraining from disclosure. This cycle allows partners to balance a need for privacy and connection.

    B.   Learning too much too soon may result in alienation. Was "too much too soon" ever the reason for terminating one of your relationships? Explain.

    _____

    _____

    C.   Self-disclosure has the greatest positive effect on relationships when it is reciprocated equally. Think about your closest relationship. Is self-disclosure equally reciprocated? Think about a relationship that has never gotten close. Describe the role of self-disclosure in that relationship.

    _____

    _____

II.   Guidelines help us to determine appropriate amounts of self-disclosure.

    A.   Self-disclose the kind of information you want others to disclose to you. Have you disclosed information with someone in order to move to a more intimate level and the partner refused to go there? Explain.

    _____

    _____

    B.   Self-disclose more intimate information only when you believe the disclosure represents an acceptable risk. Once, when I was in graduate school in France, my roommate disclosed very personal information about her marriage. I was complimented that she trusted me with the information. When we returned to the U.S., she never responded to my calls or letters. Have you ever disclosed very personal information with a stranger? Explain what happened.

    _____

    _____

C.   Continue intimate self-disclosure only if it is reciprocated. Lack of reciprocation usually means the other does not consider the relationship to be one in which extensive self-disclosure is appropriate. When my friend's husband left her, she told me that she didn't want to talk about it. Her decision not to self-disclose defined the boundaries of our friendship. Has someone you considered a friend shut you out? What effect did it have on your relationship?

D.   Move self-disclosure to deeper levels gradually. Are you someone who is fast or slow to self-disclose? Do you have a friend who is the opposite? What impact has this had on your friendship?

E.   Reserve intimate or very personal self-disclosure for ongoing relationships. People who disclose too much too soon risk alienating the other. Have you been turned off by someone's decision to disclose too much? Explain.

III.   Levels of self-disclosure and appropriateness of disclosure differ from culture to culture.

A.   Informal cultures (includes Americans) disclose more about themselves.

B.   Formal cultures (includes Germans and Japanese) disclose less. Do you know couples (one from a formal culture/one from an informal culture) who have problems that result from issues of self-disclosure?

C.   Across cultures, when relationships become more intimate, self-disclosure increases.

D.   The more partners disclose to each other, the more they are attracted to each other.

E.   Women disclose more than men. Do you have a female friend who is unwilling to self-disclose? Is she reluctant to self-disclose with all of her friends or just with you? How does it make you feel?

F.   Both men and women disclose more intimate information to women.

G.   Men in the U.S. are more likely to view conversation as report-talk: a way to share information, display knowledge, negotiate, and preserve independence.

H.   Women are more likely to see conversation as rapport-talk: a way to share experiences and establish bonds with others.

IV.   Withholding feelings is, in most instances, unhealthy.

A.   Denying feelings by keeping them inside and not giving any verbal or nonverbal cues to their existence can lead to physical problems such as ulcers and heart disease.

B.   Withholding feelings can lead to psychological problems such as stress and depression.

C.   Those who withhold are often perceived as cold, undemonstrative, and not much fun.

Describe the disclosure behavior of people in your family. Are some eager to let their feelings out? Do others have to be prodded? What about you? Do you feel that your family's display of feelings is healthy/unhealthy? Why?

_____

_____

V.   Displaying feelings, both verbally and nonverbally, reinforces our feelings.

A.   Positive displays, such as hugs, reinforce the point that we care.

B.   Displays of feelings serve as an escape valve for very strong emotions.

Describe your family's display of positive emotions. How likely are members to hug each other? Kiss each other? My father was a man who hugged, squeezed, threw me into the air, and put me up on his back. My mother was more reserved. Do members of your family vary in their display of feelings? Does their display of feelings shape how you feel about them? Explain.

_____

_____

VI.   Verbally aggressive messages that attack the self-concept of another in order to deliver psychological pain are related to physical violence (Sabourin).

A.   The less able and willing partners are to engage constructively in discussing and working through issues (argumentative skill deficiency), the more likely they are to resort to verbally aggressive messages to "win." Do you know someone involved in a verbally aggressive relationship? Are the partners unwilling to address issues?

_____

_____

B.   Partners in violent marital disagreements engage in more verbally aggressive messages than partners in nonviolent disagreements.

C.   Messages that attack the character or competence of the other person, as well as swearing and threat messages, are more likely to result in violence than are other types of verbal aggression. Do you know someone in such a relationship?

VII.   The conversations of abusive spouses differ from those of nonabusive couples.

A.   Abusive spouses are more likely to discuss relationship problems, complain, and express their own feelings.

B.   Abusive spouses have more expressions of despair.

C.   Abusive spouses complain frequently about their partners.

D.   Abusive spouses have little idea of how to go about changing what is wrong in the relationship.

E.   Both partners in an abusive relationship assert their control of the relationship by matching each other's negative behavior.

F.   Male abusers, rather than accepting responsibility for their own violence, cite their wives' behavior as the reason for their abusive behavior.

Do you know someone in an abusive relationship? Describe that person's conversational behavior.

_____

_____

VIII.   Describing feelings helps us to share our feelings with others in a manner that does not damage our relationships or cause stress.

A.   Describing feelings, by naming the emotion you are feeling without judging it, allows others to understand the effect of their behavior on you.

B. Describing feelings allows you to exercise a measure of control of others' behavior by making them aware of the effects their actions have on you.

IX. People refrain from describing their feelings for a variety of reasons.

A. Some lack a vocabulary for describing feelings such as anger, betrayal, envy, and outrage. How effective are you at finding the "right" words to identify feelings that are churning inside of you? Do you know people who hold negative feelings inside until they burst? Are you one of those people? Explain.

_____

_____

B. Some believe that describing their true feelings will make them too vulnerable. When I was in high school, I was too embarrassed to let boys know if I liked them. The result was that I dated a lot of boys who liked me but few that I liked. And you?

_____

C. Some believe that if they describe feelings, others will make them feel guilty about having such feelings. When I was in high school, I told my mother that I felt like I didn't have any privacy since my grandmother had come to live with us. My mom responded with, "Would you prefer that she was in a nursing home?" I felt terrible. Have you been made to feel guilty for honest feelings that you expressed?

_____

_____

D. Some believe that describing feelings causes harm to others or to a relationship. My best friend's husband frequently says, "YOU, AGAIN?" when I come to visit. Even though I'm almost certain he's joking, I do worry that I might have worn out my welcome. Have I ever told him about my concern? No. Can you share a similar story?

_____

_____

E. Some people come from cultures that teach them to hide their feelings and emotions from others. What have you learned from your culture concerning the display of feelings?

_____

_____

X. Follow these guidelines as you describe your feelings:

A.   Indicate what triggered the feeling.

B.   Mentally identify what you are feeling, carefully selecting the right words.

C.   Verbally own the feelings.

D.   Verbally state the specific feeling.

> For example, in IX. D: "Larry, when you say 'YOU, AGAIN?' I'm almost certain that you are teasing, but I'm concerned that I might really be bothering you."

> Think of an instance where you felt angry or hurt or vulnerable. Own your feelings and state them.

_____

_____

XI.   Owning feelings or opinions identifies you as the source of the particular idea or feeling.

A.   "I" statements help the listener understand fully and accurately the nature of the message.

B.   "I" statements identify the source of the message.

XII.   People use vague referents and avoid "I" statements for two basic reasons.

A.   They believe that vague referents like "everybody thinks" strengthen the power of their statements.

B.   They are attempting to escape responsibility. I recently told a colleague that "others" are upset with her behavior. She let me get away with it. She shouldn't have. Can you identify an "everybody thinks" comment that you recently delivered?

_____

_____

XIII.   Praising describes the specific positive behavior or accomplishment and the effect it had on others.

A.   Praise is the expression of admiration that we genuinely feel.

B.   The purpose of praise is to inform, whereas the purpose of flattery is to curry favor.

C.   Praise must focus on a specific action.

D.   The message of praise is worded so that it is in keeping with the significance or value of the accomplishment or behavior. An effective message of praise uses four guidelines:
1.   Notes the specific behavior or accomplishment.
2.   Describes the behavior or accomplishment.
3.   Describes the positive feeling that you or others experienced as a result.
4.   Appropriately reflects the significance.

I recently told a colleague, "Terry, I saw your performance of *Driving Miss Daisy* last night. Your characterization of Daisy's son was so believable. You really captured the love he felt for his mother. I was touched. Thank you for making my evening memorable." Think of someone deserving of your praise. Write the praise below using the four guidelines.

_____

_____

_____

XIV.   Constructive criticism describes specific negative behaviors or actions and the effects these behaviors have on others. Constructive criticism follows four guidelines:

A.   Describes the behavior by accurately recounting precisely what was said or done, without labeling the behavior good or bad, right or wrong.

B.   Prefaces a negative statement with a positive one whenever possible.

C.   Is as specific as possible.

D.   When appropriate, suggests how the person can change the behavior.

"Larry, last night, when I came over, you said, 'YOU, AGAIN.' When I'm at your house, you and Peggy always make me feel welcome. I think I've just been feeling insecure lately, but I'd feel better if you'd just say 'Hi'—unless, of course, I'm really bothering you. Then TELL ME!"

Think of someone to whom you would like to offer constructive criticism. Write the criticism below following the four guidelines.

_____

_____

_____

_____

XV.   We can prepare ourselves mentally to listen to constructive criticism.

   A.   Think of criticism as being in your best interest.

   B.   Before asking for constructive criticism, make sure you are ready for an honest response.

   C.   Taking the initiative to ask for constructive criticism helps avoid surprises.

XVI. You can get the constructive criticism you are looking for if you follow certain guidelines.

   A.   Specify the kind of criticism you are seeking.

   B.   Avoid negative verbal or nonverbal reactions to the criticism.

   C.   Paraphrase what you hear.

   D.   Give reinforcement to those who take your requests for criticism as honest requests.

        I asked my daughter if she thought I should take in foster children. I expected her to say, "Mom, what a great idea!" Kelly responded, "Mom, you don't have enough rules." Instead of paraphrasing to make sure I understood her criticism, I began to cry. Poor Kelly, she spent the next hour trying to convince me that any child would be lucky to call me Mom. Can you identify a time when you took constructive criticism poorly? What should you have done?

        _____

        _____

        _____

XVII. _Inter-Action Dialogue:_ Relationships move toward friendship and intimacy through appropriate self-disclosure and feedback.

   A.   Effective disclosures own opinions and describe feelings.

   B.   Effective feedback requires describing specific behavior and its effect on others.

      1.   When the effect is positive, statements of praise are used.

159

2.   When the effect is negative, constructive criticism can be given.

View your Inter-Action CD ROM and read the dialogue between Maria and Mark that is found in your text. In this dialogue, do Mark and Maria equally self-disclose? What do you think of the feedback that Maria offers Mark? Did you find it constructive or hurtful? In your opinion, is this a relationship that is on a fast track toward friendship? Explain. Is Maria the type of person you would choose as a friend? Explain.

_____

_____

_____

_____

_____

_____

_____

_____

_____

_____

Key Terms in Chapter 9
(Define each of the terms below.)

aggressive messages _____

_____

constructive criticism _____

_____

describing feelings _____

_____

displaying feelings _____

_____

flattery _____

_____

"I" statements _____

_____

owning feelings _____

_____

personal feedback _____

_____

praise _____

_____

rapport-talk _____

_____

report-talk _____

_____

self-disclosure _____

_____

withholding feelings _____

_____

Interesting Sites on the Internet

http://www.mhnet.org/psyhelp/chap13/chap13i.htm
> Sponsored by Mental Health Net, this site identifies the first two steps to overcoming the fear of self-disclosure. Material is from Clayton Tucker-Ladd's book *Psychological Self-Help*.

http://www.mhnet.org/psyhelp/chap13/chap13j.htm
> Sponsored by Mental Health Net, this site identifies steps three and four to overcoming one's fear of self-disclosure. Material is from Clayton Tucker-Ladd's book *Psychological Self-Help*.

http://ericeece.org/pubs/digests/1993/lk-sel93.html
> Sponsored by ERIC Digest, this site presents an excerpt from Lilian Katz's paper "Distinctions between Self-Esteem and Narcissism: Implications for Practice."

http://www.verbalabuse.com/7.shtml
> Cathy Hart, RN, CNM, MS Editor, identifies examples of verbal abuse in the workplace and offers suggestions for breaking the cycle.

http://www.cyberparent.com/abuse/exercise.htm
> In this site, Patricia Evans, counselor and author of *Verbal Abuse, Survivors Speak Out*, presents information about verbal abuse and offers an exercise to determine if verbal abuse is taking place.

Exercise 9.1   Name _____

Fat, I'll Tell You Who's Fat!

Purpose: To enhance your ability to describe feelings in a manner that does not damage your relationship.

Instructions:

A. Read each of the statements below.

B. Write a description of your feelings in response to each of the statements. Refrain from judging the other person. Your intent is to allow the other person to understand the effect of his/her words on you.

---

1.   (Friend)   "Is that sweater new? It makes you look fat!"
      Description:

2.   (Roommate)   "Just my luck to have a slob for a roommate!"
      Description:

3.   (Boyfriend/Girlfriend)   "I'm bored. See you later."
      Description:

4.   (Professor—responding to your question)   "Just once, try listening. You might understand what is going on in this class."
      Description:

5.   (Parent—second call for dinner)   "I said come to the dinner table NOW."
      Description:

Exercise 9.2   Name _____

What's the Word I'm Looking For?

Purpose: To enhance your ability to choose words that accurately describe your feelings.

Instructions:

A. Read the scenarios below.

B. Identify a list of words to describe what you might feel should those words be directed at you.

---

1.   Student seated next to you in class responding to grade curve on board: "What idiot couldn't manage a B on her exam?" (Your grade was C.)
Words to describe your feelings:

2.   Friend: "I'd love to go with you to the show tonight, but I'm going with Alexa. (another one of your friends)
Words to describe your feelings:

3.   Dinner guest: "I won't be asking for the recipe for this dinner. That's for sure."
Words to describe your feelings:

4.   Math professor: "I hope you aren't considering a major in math." (You are.)
Words to describe your feelings:

5.   Neighbor comes over for coffee: "It looks like you are in need of a housekeeper. Would you like the name of mine?"
Words to describe your feelings:

Exercise 9.3   Name _____

Would it Kill You to Say Something Nice?

Purpose: To enhance your ability to express praise.

Instructions:
A. Identify two people whom you admire for something that they have said or done.
B. Write a message of praise for each, making sure that the message does the following:
  1. specifies the behavior or accomplishment.
  2. describes the behavior or accomplishment.
  3. describes the positive feelings that you or others experience as a result.
C. Deliver your messages of praise.

Person #1:

Person #2:

Exercise 9.4

Name _____

What Do You Expect From a Blond?

Purpose:
1. To improve your ability to describe your feelings.
2. To increase the likelihood that you will express your feelings to the person who has offended you.

Instructions:
A. Identify two actions or behaviors of people that upset you and yet you say nothing. For example, a friend calls you "chunky cheeks" or "a dumb blond" or "airhead."
B. Identify the reason for your silence. Did you lack the right words to express your feelings? Did you feel vulnerable? Were you afraid that the other person would make you feel guilty for saying something? Were you afraid of hurting the relationship?
C. Plan your reaction in the event that the same situation might occur. Use the following guidelines:
   1. Indicate what triggered the feeling.
   2. Mentally identify what you are feeling, selecting the "right" words.
   3. Verbally own the feelings.
   4. Verbally state the specific feelings.
D. Use your planned response the next time the situation occurs.

Description #1: (Describe situation)

Reason for silence:

Response:

Description #2: (Describe situation)

Reason for silence:

Response:

Exercise 9.5

Name _____

I'm Lonely, Too

Purpose: To experience the effect that self-disclosure can have on a relationship.

Instructions:

A. Identify a "real" feeling that is private, yet one that you are willing to disclose to 3 people of your own choosing. For example: Perhaps you fear being alone or you feel unloved or unsatisfied with life. Perhaps you fear failure or not meeting up to someone else's expectations.

B. Engage in conversations with 3 different people, including your best friend, a good friend, and an acquaintance. At some point in the conversation, when the moment seems right, share your "private" feeling.

C. Record the response of each person. Did your partner react by sharing his/her own feelings on the topic? Did he/she back off? How did the partner's response make you feel? Did the "acquaintance" appear to be alienated because of "too much, too soon"?

D. Record responses below.

E. Discuss your results with a partner.

	Did/Did Not Disclose	My Reaction to His/Her Response
Best Friend		
Good Friend		
Acquaintance		

Exercise 9.6   Name _____

Ryan Made Us Laugh

Purpose: To test the hypothesis of psychologists who believe that habitually withholding feelings can be both physically and psychologically harmful.

Instructions:
A. Identify 5 people who have experienced the death of someone they love.
B. Ask them the following questions:
    1. Do you talk freely about your loss? To whom? Have listeners been receptive? After talking about the loved one who died, how do you feel?
    2. Have you developed physical or psychological problems since the death of your loved one? i.e. ulcers, sleeplessness, headaches
    3. Would you advise others who have experienced the death of a loved one to try to talk about him/her? Why?
C. Complete the chart below.
D. Discuss your findings with a partner.

	Does/Does Not Talk Freely	Listener Response	Physical / Psychological Effects	Advice
Person #1				
Person #2				
Person #3				
Person #4				
Person #5				

SELF EXAMINATION – CHAPTER 9

True/False   If false, explain what is wrong with the statement.

___ 1. People from formal cultures disclose more about themselves.

_____

___ 2. One guideline for appropriate self-disclosure says to continue intimate self-disclosure only if it is reciprocated.

_____

___ 3. The Social Penetration Theory states that relational partners consistently and predictably achieve more intimacy through self-disclosure.

_____

___ 4. The more partners disclose to each other, the more they are attracted to each other.

_____

___ 5. Constructive criticism begins by labeling the behavior as good or bad.

_____

Multiple Choice

___ 6. Which of the following is NOT true of formal cultures?
   A.   include Japanese
   B.   include Germans
   C.   include Americans
   D.   disclose less

___ 7. Which of the following statements BEST follows the guidelines set forth for giving praise?
   A.   "Damien, you were awesome in the game last night."
   B.   "Damien, I couldn't believe how many points you scored last night. You were a scoring machine!"
   C.   "Damien, your three-point shot at the buzzer was awesome."
   D.   "Damien, your performance on the court last night was the best I've ever seen."

___ 8. Which of the following is a guideline for self-disclosure?
   A.   Continue self-disclosure even if it is not reciprocated.
   B.   Move self-disclosure to deeper levels as fast as possible.
   C.   Self-disclose personal information when you feel comfortable.
   D.   Self-disclose intimate information only when disclosure represents an acceptable risk.

___ 9. Which of the following is NOT true about the levels of self-disclosure of men and women?

    A.   Women disclose more than men.

    B.   Men disclose more intimate information to women.

    C.   Women disclose more intimate information to other women.

    D.   Men in the U.S. are more likely to view conversation as rapport-talk.

___ 10. Which of the following is NOT true about the conversations of abusive spouses?

    A.   Abusive spouses are more likely to remain silent about relationship problems.

    B.   Abusive spouses have little idea of how to go about changing what is wrong with the relationship.

    C.   Both partners in an abusive relationship assert control of the relationship by matching the other's negative behavior.

    D.   Abusive spouses have more expressions of despair.

Complete the Thought

11.   "Everybody thinks" is an example of a _____ .

12.   The description of specific negative behaviors or actions and the effects this behavior has on others is known as _____ .

Essay Questions

13.   Effective constructive criticism observes four guidelines. Provide an example of effective constructive criticism and indicate where, in the criticism, you were attempting to observe each of the four guidelines.

14.   Differentiate between flattery and praise. Give an example of each.

Interpersonal Problem Solver

Someone you know is feeling low. You'd like to cheer that person up. Formulate a message that adheres to the four guidelines of effective messages of praise and share it.

Chapter 10: Using Interpersonal Influence Ethically

Interactive Chapter Outline

I.   Influence is the process of changing the attitudes and/or actions of others.

      A.   Historically, influence was called persuasion.

      B.   Understanding influence processes and learning how to use influence ethically are fundamental to effectiveness in relationships.

When I was six, my best friend, Judy, convinced me that I should kneel on a piece of glass to prove how brave I was. After significant blood loss and tears, I realized that I wasn't particularly brave. In fifth grade, my good friend Susan told me to hold my body stiff and fall backwards, promising that she'd catch me. She didn't. One broken right arm later, I realized that I shouldn't have trusted Susan. Who is your most influential friend? Has that friend influenced you to do something ethical/unethical? Explain.

_____

_____

_____

_____

_____

_____

_____

II.   Interpersonal power is the potential a person has in a relationship to influence another's attitudes, beliefs, and behaviors.

      A.   People with strong power bases are more effective at influencing others.

      B.   People perceived as more expert, attractive, trustworthy, and credible are more likely to be persuasive. Who, in your life, has the greatest interpersonal power? Explain.

_____

_____

_____

_____

_____

III.   Five major sources of power exist in relationships.

   A.   Coercive power exists if one is able to harm another physically and/or psychologically should the other resist the influence attempt. Do you know a woman or man who has remained in an unhealthy relationship because of the coercive (whether real or perceived) power of a partner? Have you?

   B.   Reward power exists if one is able to provide monetary, physical, or psychological benefits that the partner desires.

   In 5th grade, my friend Susan convinced me to walk her home every day with the promise of a bite of the Twinkie or Suzy-Q she planned to purchase at the corner store. Who, among your friends, has reward power over you? What is that reward and how powerful is it? In your relationship, what have you been willing to do in order to receive that reward? Has reward power had a positive or negative effect on your relationship?

   _____

   _____

   _____

   _____

   _____

   Do you know friends locked in unhealthy relationships because of the reward power of sex? Drugs? A sense of feeling needed? Explain.

   _____

   _____

   _____

   _____

   _____

   C.   Legitimate power exists if one can use the status that comes from being elected, selected, or from holding a position to influence a partner. Do you perceive your parents as having legitimate power over you resulting from their status as "mother" and "father"? Explain.

   _____

   _____

   _____

In your relationships, whom do you consider to have the greatest "legitimate power" over you right now? Explain.

_____

_____

_____

_____

D.   Expert power exists if one has knowledge that the relational partner does not have. Are you in a relationship where you must frequently defer to your partner because you lack the knowledge to disagree? Explain.

_____

_____

_____

_____

E.   Referent power exists if you are attracted to your partner due to physical appearance, image, charisma, or personality.

Consider past romantic relationships. Did you ever date someone because he/she was class president? Prom queen/king? Most popular? Most attractive? Did that person's referent power affect your relationship? If so, how?

_____

_____

_____

_____

Identify two people who are significant in your life. Discuss their "power" and the effect that that power has on your relationship.

_____

_____

_____

_____

_____

_____

IV.   Persuasion is the intentional verbal attempt to influence the attitudes or behaviors of others using ethical means.

    A.   Ethical means to rely primarily on argumentation rather than force.

    B.   Ethical persuasion involves the use of reasons that have an impact on the person(s) you are trying to influence.

V.   Persuasion involves giving good reasons.

    A.   Reasons are statements that provide the basis or cause for some behavior or action. They are ethically important because they provide a rational basis for a claim and provide the basis for our decision whether or not to comply.

    B.   Claims are statements of belief or a request for action. Claims are backed up with reasons. If a friend were to claim, "You need a break," the friend would back up the claim with reasons. (Reason #1) "You've had your head buried in that interpersonal communication book for the past hour. (Reason #2) You must be bored to death!" Since Reason #2 is obviously "irrational," the listener is unlikely to comply. (Right?)

VI.   Good reasons have common characteristics.

    A.   Good reasons are relevant to the claim. If you are encouraging a friend to enroll in Interpersonal Communication next semester, you would focus on course criteria important to that friend. What would those criteria be?

        _____

        _____

    B.   Good reasons are well supported. If you claim that Interpersonal Communication is a course that has improved your friendships, what support would you offer?

        _____

        _____

    C.   Good reasons focus on aspects that will have the greatest impact on the person you're trying to influence. If you know that your friend hates exams and if the majority of the course grade in Interpersonal Communication is based on a research paper and class projects, then emphasize the limited role of exams. What aspect of this course would have the greatest impact on your friend? Why?

        _____

        _____

VII. Good reasons become more persuasive when presented by a credible source.

    A.   Credibility is the extent to which a source is perceived as competent, trustworthy, and likable.

    B.   Lack of confidence in a person may be sufficient reason not to believe the person. Is there someone whom you would "never" believe? Why?

    _____

    _____

    _____

    C.   If a person is "our hero" we may be tempted to believe whatever the person says without reasons. Who is your "hero"(you wouldn't question his/her recommendation) when it comes to choosing a movie? Going out on a blind date? Believing that something looks good on you?

    _____

    _____

    _____

VIII. The ELM theory of persuasion (Elaboration Likelihood Model) says that attitude change is likely to occur through one of two relatively distinct "routes of persuasion." (Petty)

    A.   The central route of persuasion is through a person's careful and thoughtful consideration of the true merits of the information presented in support of a claim. What have you come to believe having followed this route?

    _____

    _____

    B.   The peripheral route is via a simple cue in the persuasion context (such as an attractive source) that induces change without necessitating scrutiny of the central merits of the claim. I started using a new brand of hair color simply because my friend "with beautiful hair" said that the color would be perfect for me. When was the last time you took the peripheral route in making a decision? Why? Were you glad?

    _____

    _____

    C.   The ELM hypothesizes that what is persuasive to a person depends on how motivated and able the person is to access the merits of a speaker, an issue, or a position.

1. The highly motivated person studies available information about a claim to arrive at a reasoned attitude (central route). The attitude change usually results in a behavioral change.
2. The less motivated gather their information through less resource-demanding processes (peripheral route). The attitude change seldom results in a behavioral change.

I chose the peripheral route when buying my car. I saw the Acura when I was helping my daughter buy her car. Kelly said, "Mom, you'd look great in that car." So much for research. I bought it. Think about your most recent "big purchase." Did you follow the central or peripheral route in deciding what to buy?

_____

_____

IX. A credible source possesses the following qualities:

A. Credible sources are competent. They seem to know what they are talking about, seem to have good information, and are perceived as clear thinkers. The more you are perceived as competent, the more likely it is that someone will pay attention to your views.

Jim is my competent source for investments, Bob for a "different" perspective, and Sue for compassion. Identify some of your competent sources.

_____

_____

B. Credible sources are trustworthy. They seem to be dependable and honest, keep promises, and act for the good of others.

To whom do you turn for an honest opinion about a problem in a dating relationship? Why?

_____

_____

_____

C. Credible sources are likable. Likable people are congenial, attractive, warm, and friendly. Have you ever been taken in by a scam artist who cultivated personal characteristics just to get something out of you? Explain.

_____

_____

_____

X.   Credibility can be cultivated.

    A.   Show that you know what you are doing and why. Taking on too many tasks with too little time to complete any of them may give the impression of incompetence. As I'm writing this manual I'm also teaching a full load of classes. I spoke French in my Speech class yesterday! (I teach in two disciplines.) I can still see the eyes of the students saying, "What the heck???"

    B.   Show that you care about the effects on others of what you say and do. People get labeled "manipulators" for failing to state their intentions.

    C.   Behave in ways that are ethical. Presidential candidate McCain expressed that it was ethically wrong for George W. Bush to speak at Bob Jones University, a school with a policy that forbade interracial dating and whose founder is said to have made anti-Catholic statements. McCain's ethical goal of informing the public appeared to take an unethical turn when McCain's staff (supposedly) referred to Bush as "anti-Catholic." Have you ever considered behaving in an unethical way to achieve an ethical goal? Explain.

    _____

    _____

XI.   Ethical persuasion demands certain behaviors.

    A.   Tell the truth. If people believe you are lying, they are likely to reject you and your ideas. Is there someone you refuse to believe? Why?

    _____

    _____

    B.   Resist personal attacks against those who oppose your ideas. Name-calling is detrimental to trustworthiness. Have you ever resorted to personal attacks? Why? What was the result?

    _____

    _____

    C.   Disclose the complete picture. Putting a favorable spin on unfavorable information is unethical. My friend convinced me to go on a blind date by telling me that the man was kind, compassionate, nice looking, well-educated, and lonely. She failed to mention that he talked incessantly. Are you guilty of a similar "oversight?"

XII.   In order to influence someone to act, emotional involvement is crucial.

    A.   The effectiveness of emotional appeals depends on such factors as mood and attitude of the person you are persuading.

B. The effectiveness of emotional appeals depends on the language itself.

C. Reason and emotion are inseparable in a persuasive message. Identify a reasonable yet emotional appeal that you might use to convince your professor to delay an exam.

XIII. Compliance Gaining strategies focus on getting others to behave the way you want them to.

A. Supporting-evidence strategies draw primarily on reason. "Come with me to the bar tonight. The band plays your favorite music."

B. Exchange strategies include trade-offs. "If you come with me to the bar tonight, I'll go to the play with you next week."

C. Direct-request strategies ask another to behave in a particular way. They are based primarily on credibility and are not accompanied with reasons. "Would you come to the bar with me tonight?"

D. Empathy-based strategies seek compliance by appealing to another's love, affection, or sympathy. "It wouldn't be any fun at the bar without you. You wouldn't let me down, would you?"

E. Face-maintenance strategies use indirect messages and emotion-eliciting statements. "Man, I hate going alone to the bar."

F. Other-benefit strategies identify behaviors that benefit the other person. "I think you need a chance to unwind tonight. Want to join me at the bar?"

G. Distributive strategies seek compliance by threatening or making the person feel guilty. "If you don't love me enough to go to bed with me, then maybe we should just end this relationship right now."

Choose your own topic and apply each of the compliance-gaining strategies.

_____

_____

_____

_____

_____

_____

XIV.   Guidelines help to determine which compliance-gaining strategy to use.

   A.   Choose the strategy that is most likely to be effective. Think about the particular listener's preferences.

   B.   Choose the strategy that will best protect the relationship. If the relationship is an important one, you do not want to appear manipulative.

   C.   Choose the strategy that is most comfortable for you.

        Think of something you would like your best friend to do. Identify the strategy that you think is best and write it out.

        _____

        _____

        _____

XV.   When an individual's rights are ignored or violated he/she may respond in one of three ways. The appropriate response depends upon the situation.

   A.   Passive behavior is displayed by people reluctant to state their opinions, share feelings, or assume responsibility for their actions. Rather than influence, people submit. Describe your most memorable "passive" behavior. Why were you reluctant to speak?

        _____

        _____

        _____

   B.   Aggressive behavior is displayed by people who lash out at the source of their discontent with little regard for the situation or for the feelings, needs, or rights of those they are attacking. Describe your most memorable aggressive behavior. Why do you think you behaved aggressively? What was the outcome?

        _____

        _____

        _____

   C.   Assertive behavior is displayed by people who stand up for themselves in an interpersonally effective way. I recently spoke to five employees of AT&T in an attempt to have one of them agree to erase a $140 phone bill that I had received for calling card minutes I had been told were free. The fifth person agreed. Describe your most memorable assertive behavior. Did something positive result?

_____

_____

_____

_____

XVI. Assertive speakers observe the following rules:

A. Own their ideas, thoughts, and feelings.

B. Describe behavior and feelings.

C. Maintain eye contact and a self-confident posture.

D Use a firm but pleasant tone of voice.

E. Avoid vocalized pauses.

F. Are sensitive to the face needs of the others.

When I'm involved in a "disagreement" with another, I frequently violate the rules for posture and voice: I tense my body and increase my volume. Which of the above rules do you violate most often? Describe a time when your violation of one of these rules caused a disagreement to escalate.

_____

_____

_____

_____

_____

_____

XVII. Guidelines should be followed when practicing assertive behavior.

A. Identify what you are thinking or feeling.

B. Analyze the cause of these feelings.

C. Choose the appropriate skills to communicate these feelings and achieve the outcome you desire.

D. Communicate these feelings to the appropriate person.

Identify a problem that you need to address. Shape an assertive statement and deliver it to the appropriate person.

XVIII. Cultures have different attitudes concerning assertive behavior.

A. Assertive behavior is practiced primarily in Western cultures.

B. Asian cultures may view maintaining "face" and politeness to be more important than achieving satisfaction through assertive behavior.

C. Latin and Hispanic societies exercise a highly assertive male behavior referred to as "machismo."

D. Failure to understand cultural attitudes may lead to fear and misunderstanding.

Have you experienced a situation in which your assertive behavior was viewed as aggressive or your passive behavior was viewed as weak? Explain.

_____

_____

_____

_____

_____

XIX. *Inter-Action Dialogue.* Influence occurs when one person attempts to change another person's attitudes or actions. Influence takes several forms:

A. Reasons and evidence

B. Credibility

C. Emotional appeal

D. Compliance-gaining strategies

E. Assertiveness

View this dialogue on your Inter-Action CD ROM and read the script in your text. When Paul learns that Hannah has purchased a term paper, what word does he use to describe her behavior? What form of influence is he using? Do you think it was an effective form of influence? What do you think of Paul's use of reasons and evidence? Which reason, if any, did you find to be the most influential? Did you find it credible when Hannah agreed to write her own paper? In your opinion, which of Paul's attempts at influence proved to be the most effective? Explain.

_____

_____

_____

_____

_____

_____

_____

_____

_____

_____

_____

_____

_____

Key Terms in Chapter 10
(Define each of the terms below.)

aggressive behavior _____

_____

assertive behavior _____

_____

claims _____

_____

coercive power _____

_____

competence _____

_____

compliance gaining _____

_____

credibility _____

_____

direct-request strategies _____

_____

distributive strategies _____

_____

elaboration likelihood model _____

_____

empathy-based strategies _____

_____

exchange strategies _____

_____

expert power _____

_____

face-maintenance strategies _____

_____

influence _____

_____

legitimate power _____

_____

likeability _____

_____

other-benefit strategies _____

_____

passive behavior _____

_____

persuasion _____

_____

reasons _____

_____

referent power _____

_____

reward power _____

_____

social power _____

_____

supporting-evidence strategies _____

_____

trustworthiness _____

_____

Interesting Sites on the Internet

http://www.hsc.edu/stu/counseling/selfhelp/assert.html
    The Counseling Center at Hampden-Sydney College offers helpful hints for assertive
    behavior.
http://www2.ag.ohio-state.edu/ ~ ohioline/hyg-fact/5000/5289.html
    Joan Reid, Ohio State University, explores the important role that feelings play in daily
    communication. She references *The Power of Ethical Persuasion* by Dr. Tom Rusk.
http://www.rickross.com/reference/brainwashing/brainwashing8.html
    In this site, taken from *Encyclopedia of Sociology Vol. 1*, Richard J. Ofshe, Ph.D.,
    discusses coercive persuasion and thought reform.
http://www.as.wvu.edu/ ~ sbb/comm221/chapters/judge.htm
    Steve Booth-Butterfield, professor of Persuasion Theory and Research, explains how
    the Social Judgment Theory offers powerful guidelines for persuasion.
http://ici2.umn.edu/preschoolbehavior/tip_sheets/passagg.htm
    This site, sponsored by the University of Minnesota, offers positive ways of preventing
    and dealing with passive-aggressive behavior.

Exercise 10.1

Name _____

Come Fly With Me

Purpose: To increase your awareness of the "routes of persuasion" you follow as you allow your attitude to change.

Instructions:

A. Review Petty's ELM theory that defines two "routes of persuasion." The central route of persuasion is through a person's careful and thoughtful consideration of the true merits of the information. The peripheral route is via a simple cue in the persuasion context that induces change without scrutinizing the merits of the claim.

B. List below three recent efforts used by others to change your attitude. Ask yourself, "Did I follow a 'central' or 'peripheral' route in arriving at my decision?" Label your response as 'central' or 'peripheral.'

> The attractive student seated next to you in class says, "Would you like to join me for coffee in the Student Union? We could review for the exam." Did you make your decision to go on the peripheral route of "looks" or the central route of "He/she is an A student who could help me do better on the exam"?

C. Discuss with a partner your findings. Do you find yourself typically following a central or peripheral route? Why? Does this result in problems?

Persuasive Effort #1:

My Response:

Persuasive Effort #2:

My Response:

Persuasive Effort #3:

My Response:

Exercise 10.2   Name _____

I'd Buy a Used Car From Her

Purpose: To examine the role that credibility plays in decision-making.

Instructions:

A. Credibility is the extent to which we perceive someone as competent, trustworthy, and likable. Think about the people in your life whom you view most credible.

B. Identify one person in each of the following categories whom you regard as "most credible" and one whom you regard as "least credible."
   1. Teacher   2. Friend   3. Business acquaintance

C. Identify the characteristics that cause you to regard each person as "most credible" and "least credible."

D. Discuss with a partner the criteria most important to you in determining credibility. Is something missing from your list? Do you have a good track record for judging people? How often have you been burned?

Most Credible Teacher:

Characteristics:

Least Credible Teacher:

Characteristics:

Most Credible Friend:

Characteristics:

Least Credible Friend:

Characteristics:

Most Credible Business Acquaintance:

Characteristics:

Least Credible Business Acquaintance:

Characteristics:

Exercise 10.3

Name _____

I'd Follow You Anywhere

Purpose: To increase your skill at choosing the appropriate compliance gaining strategy in order to get others to behave as you want.

Instructions:

A. Identify three behaviors you would like to elicit from each of the following: a friend, a parent, a professor.
B. Decide on the appropriate compliance gaining strategy to use in order to get what you want.
C. Write out a dialogue to accompany the strategy you select.
    1. Friend: Backpack through Europe.   Strategy: Supporting-evidence
    2. Dialogue: "Kashan, I'd love to have you go with me to Europe. We could visit the cities where your mother and father were born. We could look up some of your relatives. I know how much you've wanted to connect with family."
D. Use your strategy.
E. With a partner discuss the following: What worked and why? What didn't work and why? What should you have said and why?

_____

Friend: Strategy:
Dialogue:

Professor: Strategy:
Dialogue:

Parent: Strategy:
Dialogue:

Exercise 10.4   Name _____

Walk on Water? For You? Sure!

Purpose: To increase your ability to back up claims with good reasons.

Instructions:
A. Review text research on good reasons.
B. Choose an action that you sincerely want your friend to do with or for you.
C. Identify the "good reasons" that will have the greatest impact on your friend. Make sure the reasons are relevant to the claim and well-supported.
D. Discuss with a partner the outcome of your exercise. How effective was your reasoning? What worked? What didn't? Why?

_____

Request: _____

Brainstorm: Compile a list of arguments that might cause your friend to comply with your request. Choose the best and list them below. Make sure each reason is well-supported.

Reason #1:

Reason #2:

Reason #3:

Reason #4:

Exercise 10.5   Name _____

Because You're So Darn Good Lookin', That's Why

Purpose: To enhance your power of persuasion.

Instructions:
A. Acquaint yourself with the following two routes of persuasion as set forth in the Elaboration Likelihood Model theory of persuasion (ELM):
   1. The central route of persuasion is through a person's careful and thoughtful consideration of the true merits of the information presented in support of a claim.
   2. The peripheral route is via a simple cue that induces change minus scrutiny of the merits of a claim.
B. In the space below, use a central route of persuasion and a peripheral route of persuasion to argue each of the following:
   1. Persuade a friend to enroll in this course next semester.
   2. Persuade a student in your class to treat you to lunch.
   3. Persuade your best friend to loan you $50.

FRIEND

Central Route:

Peripheral Route:

STUDENT

Central Route:

Peripheral Route:

BEST FRIEND

Central Route:

Peripheral Route:

Exercise 10.6   Name _____

It Must Be True. Tom Brokaw Wouldn't Lie.

Purpose: To increase an awareness of the factors that lead us to label someone as credible.

Instructions:

A. Identify 5 people whom you like and trust and whom you believe to be credible sources on a particular topic, such as "who masterminded the events of September 11?"
B. Do as much reading as possible on the topic you select.
C. Write 10 questions concerning the topic that you have chosen. Make sure that you have answers to each of the questions you ask. For example: "Do you know how many of the men who commandeered the planes that crashed into the Pentagon and the Twin Towers were Iraqi?"
D. Pose the 10 questions to each of the 5 people.
E. Decide which one of the 5 people you found most credible and why. What role did affection and trust play in your decision? Was your determination of credibility linked to the person's willingness to say "I don't know," or were you more inclined to believe the person who had an answer for everything? Were you tempted to believe someone even if he/she couldn't tell you where he/she got the answer? Did you even bother to ask?

Identify whom you found "most credible." Explain why.

SELF EXAMINATION – CHAPTER 10

True/False   If false, explain what is wrong with the statement.

___ 1. Credibility is the extent to which a source is perceived as competent, trustworthy, and likable.

_____

___ 2. Face-maintenance compliance-gaining strategies use indirect messages.

_____

___ 3. Claims are statements that provide the basis or cause for some behavior or action.

_____

___ 4. Persuasion is the intentional verbal attempt to influence the attitudes or behaviors of others using any means available.

_____

___ 5. The ELM theory says that attitude change is likely to occur only through a person's careful and thoughtful consideration of the true merits of the information presented in support of a claim.

_____

Multiple Choice

6. Which of the following answers includes the three qualities of a credible source?
    A.   trustworthy, competent, and direct
    B.   trustworthy, kind, and direct
    C.   competent, likeable, and direct
    D.   competent, trustworthy, and likable

7. Which of the following methods is most likely to be used by an unmotivated person gathering information about a claim?
    A.   central route
    B.   central and peripheral route
    C.   peripheral route
    D.   none of the above

8. Which of the following is NOT true of ethical persuasion?
    A.   puts favorable spin on unfavorable information
    B.   is always truthful
    C.   resists personal attacks
    D.   discloses the complete picture

9. Which of the following best defines coercive power?
    A. derived from a person's ability to give or withhold tangible goods
    B. derived from having knowledge in a specific field
    C. derived from a person's position of power
    D. derived from the belief that a person can harm us if we assert ourselves

10. Which of the following is NOT a rule observed by assertive speakers.
    A. use specific statements directed to the behaviors
    B. maintain a firm tone of voice
    C. speak clearly
    D. maintain a relaxed body position

Complete the Thought

11. People who lash out at the source of their discontent with little regard for the situation or feelings of those they attack are termed _____.

12. People who stand up for themselves in an interpersonally effective way are termed _____.

Essay Questions

13. Good reasons have common characteristics. Explain. Provide a claim and back it up with good reasons that address the characteristics cited.

14. Verderber and Verderber cite seven compliance-gaining strategies that focus on getting others to behave the way you want them to. Explain them and apply and label each strategy in the following situation: You are headed to Mexico for Spring Break with three friends with whom you went to high school. You'd love to have your roommate come along but she/he thinks it would be awkward since she/he doesn't know your friends.

Interpersonal Problem Solver

Close your eyes and picture the one person in your life who, at the moment, seems to hold the greatest power over you. Based upon your knowledge of the five major sources of power in relationships, analyze why you believe this person has so much power over you.

Chapter 11: Managing Conflict

Interactive Chapter Outline

I.   The perception of interpersonal conflict is culturally based.

    A.   Interpersonal conflict is a situation in which the needs or ideas of one person are perceived to be at odds with or in opposition to the needs or ideas of another.

    B.   From an American perspective, conflict is not a negative phenomenon.

    C.   Other cultures, especially Asian, view conflict as dysfunctional to relationships and damaging to social face. Have you engaged in conflict with someone from another culture? Explain.

        _____

        _____

II.   Recognizing the type of conflict can sometimes resolve it before it escalates.

    A.   A pseudoconflict is apparent, not real. It is a conflict waiting to happen. There are two types of pseudoconflicts.

        1.   Badgering includes teasing and taunting. It can be destructive when the goal is to goad the partner into a fight. My son used to hold his sister on the floor and pretend that he was going to let drool drop on her face. When the drool "accidentally" dropped, all hell broke loose. Describe your "taunting" behavior.

            _____

            _____

        2.   A pseudoconflict occurs when partners believe desired results cannot be achieved simultaneously when they really can. My son and daughter didn't like pizza. My husband wanted to go out once a week to Drag's for their large thin-crust Supreme. The kids whined about going out, and my husband's feelings were always hurt that his children were so ungrateful. The conflict subsided when Terry and I started ordering hamburgers for the children and pizza for us. (Duh, what a no-brainer!) Can you think of a similar "no-brainer?"

            _____

            _____

III. Conflicts are resolvable.

    A. Fact conflict or simple conflict is conflict concerning message accuracy. The information needed to resolve the conflict is easy to get. Disengage from the conflict until the source needed to verify facts can be found.

    B. Value conflicts are conflicts over the deep-seated beliefs people hold about what is good and bad.
        1. The conflict management for these is more difficult. The less congruence between value hierarchies, the more likely two people will experience value conflicts.
        2. At times you may have to agree to disagree.
        3. Resolution begins with the recognition that the issue is a value conflict. For example, while I believe that deer hunting with a gun is inhumane and personally choose not to hunt, both of my children hunt. What value conflicts occur in your family?

        4. Use other values on which you agree in order to arrive at a mutually satisfying resolution. Has your family resolved their value conflicts by arriving at a mutually satisfying resolution?

    C. Policy conflicts occur when two people disagree about what should be the appropriate plan, course of action, or behavior in dealing with a perceived problem. My husband believed it was disrespectful for the children to swear at their mother and that swearing merited punishment. I accepted swearing as "part of the argument." Did your family have similar policy conflicts?

        1. Because policy conflicts concern what "should" be done, there are no "right" or "wrong" behaviors and policy arrives as a result of agreement.
        2. If a problem-solving approach is not used, policy conflicts escalate into ego conflicts. My husband decided that I should stop using the credit card. I said, "I only use the credit card when there isn't enough money in the checkbook." No problem-solving approach was used. Instead, this issue escalated into an ego conflict. Do you have a similar story?

    D. Ego conflicts occur when the people involved view "winning" or "losing" the conflict as central to maintaining their positive self-image.
        1. Both people see the conflict as a measure of who they are, what they are, how competent they are, whom they have power over, or how much they

know. My husband saw himself as an excellent money manager. I saw myself as frugal.

2. "Winning" is the only means of satisfying needs.

3. Discussion of facts or values is undermined by personal or judgmental statements. When the credit card bill arrived, my husband would look at it and say, "I thought you weren't going to use this credit card." I wonder where he got that idea?

4. The more competent you are on the issue, the more likely you are to become ego-involved when your word is questioned. We both knew that we were "right," and neither of us was about to change our position.

5. When an ego-conflict is brewing, try to move it back down to a fact level. Initially, I explained each purchase on the credit card bill to my husband and why each purchase was crucial.

6. Your ability to remain rational is lost and emotions take over.

When my husband questioned my use of the credit card, I felt like I was being treated like a child. He felt out of control. Voilà, ego-conflict. Can you share a similar story?

_____

_____

IV. The five styles of conflict management differ in their outcomes.

A. Withdrawal is the easiest way to deal with conflict.
1. People physically or psychologically remove themselves from the conflict.
2. This method is both uncooperative and unassertive because at least one person refuses to talk.
3. Psychological withdrawal occurs when one person simply ignores what the other is saying.
4. Withdrawal creates a lose/lose situation because neither accomplishes what he or she wants.
5. Withdrawal leads to relationship decline because the conflict does not get managed.
6. Withdrawal results in mulling behavior. The person perceives the conflict as more severe and begins engaging in blaming behavior.
7. Bruce Jacobs suggests that withdrawal is responsible for racial rage. Race has become so toxic a topic that people refuse to address the issue. For example, I'm Caucasian. Once, in an Oral Interpretation class, I read a poem to my students which was written by Gwendolyn Brooks. An African-American student stared at me with a look of hatred. After class I asked him, "What is wrong?" "Nothing!" "Please, something is wrong—tell me." His anger exploded, "That's my poetry, NOT yours."

8.   Withdrawal is useful in two instances.
    a.   Withdrawal is useful when it permits a temporary disengagement whose purpose is to let the heat subside. The withdrawer should make his/her reason for withdrawal clear.
    b.   Withdrawal is appropriate when neither the relationship nor the issue is really important.

Have you withdrawn in anger? Explain.

_____

_____

B.   Accommodating is a form of conflict management in which people attempt to satisfy others' needs while neglecting their own.
    1.   This approach is cooperative but unassertive. It preserves friendly relationships.
    2.   Habitual accommodating reveals an unwillingness to assert one's position, resulting in lack of critical appraisal and failure to protect personal rights.
    3.   People insecure in a relationship will do anything to avoid conflict.
    4.   Accommodation is win/lose since one side gets what it wants and the other side gives up.
    5.   Accommodation may lead to poor decision making since important facts, arguments, and positions are not voiced.
    6.   Habitual accommodation results in one person taking advantage of the other, which can lead to resentment and a damaged self-concept.
    7.   Accommodating is appropriate when the issue is not important to you but the relationship is.
    8.   To the Japanese, accommodation is thought to be more humble and face-saving than the risk of losing respect through conflict.

My work-study student was having trouble saying "no." I had a heart-to-heart conversation with her, explaining that others were likely to take advantage of her. I told her she needed to actually practice saying "no." The conversation ended, and we got back to work. When I told her that I needed several articles photocopied right away, she looked at me and said, "No, I have to get going." Victory? I guess. Do you know someone who accommodates? Explain. Do you feel as though you take advantage of this person? Explain.

_____

_____

C.   Forcing or competing is a form of conflict management in which people attempt to satisfy their own needs or advance their own ideas.
    1.   No concern is shown for the needs or ideas of others.
    2.   No concern is shown for the harm done to the relationship.

3. Forcing involves physical threats, verbal attacks, coercion, or manipulation. When the other accommodates, conflict subsides. If not, conflict escalates.

4. Forcing, from an individual-satisfaction standpoint, is win/lose. The side with power claims victory. From a relational standpoint, forcing usually hurts a relationship.

5. Forcing is effective in two instances.

   a. Forcing is effective in emergencies, when quick and decisive action is crucial.

   b. Forcing is effective when interacting with someone who will take advantage of you if you do not force the issue.

Are you aware of a relationship where the partner typically uses force to manage conflict? Explain.

_____

_____

D. Compromising is a form of conflict management in which people attempt to resolve their conflict by providing at least some satisfaction for both parties.

1. Both give up part of what they really want or trade to get.

2. Compromising requires some assertiveness and some cooperation.

3. From a personal-satisfaction standpoint, compromise is lose/lose. The quality of the decision is affected if one party "trades away" a better solution.

4. From a relational-satisfaction standpoint, compromise is neutral to positive. Both parties gain.

5. Compromising is appropriate when the issue is moderately important, when there are time constraints, and when attempts at forcing or collaborating haven't worked.

When was the last time you compromised your position? Do you agree that from a personal-satisfaction standpoint, you and your partner lost? Explain.

_____

_____

E. Collaborating is a form of conflict management in which people try to fully address the needs and issues of each party and arrive at a solution that is mutually satisfying.

1. Collaborating is assertive because both parties voice their concerns.

2. Collaborating is cooperative because both parties work together to gain resolution.

3. From an individual-satisfaction point, collaborating is win/win because both sides gain from the process.

4. From a relational-satisfaction standpoint, collaboration is positive because both sides are heard.
5. This style requires accurate, precise language to describe ideas and feelings.
6. This style requires empathic listening to ideas and feelings.
7. This style requires a problem-solving approach. Partners must define and analyze the problem, develop acceptable criteria for judging alternative solutions, suggest possible solutions, and select the best solution and work to implement it.

Describe your most recent collaborating experience. Was the process satisfying? What role did empathic listening play? How hard is it for you to listen in conflict situations?

_____

_____

_____

V. Communication skills and verbal strategies aid in resolving conflict.

A. Canary's research consistently shows that the primary goal in managing conflict is to show competence that is both appropriate and effective.
1. Appropriate behaviors are marked by agreement.
2. Effective behaviors include stating complete arguments, elaborating and justifying one's point of view, and clearly developing ideas.
3. Competent communicators "frame" the interaction as one of cooperative problem solving by first acknowledging the other's viewpoint or agreeing with part of the other's argument before explaining, justifying, and arguing their viewpoint.

"Ryan, I agree that you need a vehicle that you can trust to get you to work. But I think that it would be a mistake for you to buy the Blazer. The monthly payment, together with rent and living expenses, will leave you with nothing for entertainment." Describe the most recent "appropriate and effective" arguments someone has used on you lately.

_____

_____

VI. Guidelines should be followed when initiating conflict.

A. Recognize and state ownership of the apparent problem. "Kelly, I felt bad last night when I heard you joking with Amy about how I try to run your life."

B.   Describe the basis of the potential conflict in terms of behavior, consequences, and feelings (b-c-f). "I'm worried that you were serious."

C.   Avoid evaluating the other person's motives.

D.   Be sure the other person understands your problem.

E.   Think of exactly what you will say before you confront the other person, so that your request will be brief and precise.

F.   Phrase your request in a way that focuses on common ground. "Please tell me when I do something that you find controlling. We will both be a lot happier if we can talk about it."

Are you presently "upset" with someone? Initiate a conflict conversation using the above guidelines.

_____

_____

VII.   Responding effectively to conflict requires basic communication skills.

A.   Accurately reading nonverbal cues can help to defuse a conflict.
    1.   Affirming nonverbals include smiling, pleasant facial expression, eye contact, wide and bright eyes, touch, close proximity, leaning in, relaxed body posture, nodding, gesturing, appearing calm/relaxed, peppy and upbeat voice, warm and sincere voice, and vocal expressiveness.
    2.   Unaffirming nonverbal behaviors escalate conflict. They include tense/frowning face or blank facial expression, grinding teeth, stern/staring eyes, no eye contact, increased proximity, rigid/jittery body, clenched fists, crossed arms, touch avoidance, shaky or stuttering voice, and loud voice.

B.   Put your "shields up" rather than become defensive and blindly counterattack.
    1.   Remind yourself that it is the other person who has a problem, not you.
    2.   Remind yourself that the reaction is probably an accumulation of frustration.

C.   Respond empathically with genuine interest and concern.
    1.   Be attentive. Sometimes, you just need to allow others time to vent.
    2.   Only when the other has calmed down should you begin to problem-solve.

D.   Paraphrase your understanding of the problem, and ask questions to clarify issues.

E.   Seek common ground by finding some aspect of the complaint to agree with.

F.   Ask the person to suggest alternatives.

Students tell me that my eyes shine like knives when I'm attacked. What unaffirming nonverbal behavior do you emit?

_____

_____

VIII.   Mediators can help to resolve conflicts if they observe guidelines.

A.   Make sure people agree to work with you.

B.   Help the people identify the real conflict.

C.   Maintain neutrality.

D.   Keep the discussion focused on the issues rather than on personalities.

E.   Work to ensure equal airtime.

F.   Focus the discussion on finding solutions, not placing blame.

G.   Make sure both parties fully understand and support the agreed-upon solution.

H.   Establish an action plan and follow-up procedure.

How frequently do friends call upon you to serve as a mediator? Why/Why not? To whom do you turn when you are looking for a mediator? Why?

_____

_____

_____

IX.   We can learn from unresolved conflicts.

A.   Ask yourself questions: "Where did things go wrong?" "What caused the defensiveness?" "Did I use a style that was inappropriate?"

B.   Analysis puts us in a better position to be successful the next time.

Describe an unresolved conflict in your life. Where did things go wrong? What could you have done differently to change the outcome? Is it too late?

_____

_____

_____

X.   _Inter-Action Dialogue:_ Conflict occurs when the needs of one person are perceived to be at odds with or in opposition to the needs or ideas of another.

   A.   Particular management styles help to resolve conflict.

   B.   Particular communication skills promote successful conflict management.

   Refer to Brian and Matt's conversation in Chapter 11 of your text. Throughout this conversation, Brian uses several styles of conflict management. Identify where, if at all, he uses the following: Withdrawal? Accommodation? Forcing? Compromise? Collaboration?

   Withdrawal: _____

   Accommodation: _____

   Forcing: _____

   Compromise: _____

   Collaboration: _____

   At what point in the conversation is Brian most effective at communicating the real conflict? At what point in the conversation is Brian least effective at promoting successful conflict management? Explain.

   _____

   _____

   _____

   _____

   _____

   If you were Brian, how might you have handled this conversation differently in order to resolve the conflict?

   _____

   _____

   _____

   _____

   _____

Key Terms in Chapter 11
(Define each of the terms below.)

accommodating _____

_____

collaborating _____

_____

compromising _____

_____

ego conflict _____

_____

face conflict _____

_____

forcing _____

_____

interpersonal conflict _____

_____

mediator _____

_____

policy conflict _____

_____

pseudoconflict _____

_____

shield _____

_____

value conflict _____

_____

withdrawal _____

_____

Interesting Sites on the Internet

http://www.mediate.com/articles/afccstds.cfm

> Pepperdine University School of Law sponsors this site, which describes the Model Standards of Practice for Family and Divorce Mediation.

http://www.nocompromise.org/

> Sponsored by *NO COMPROMISE* (a militant, direct-action magazine of grassroots animal liberationists and supporters), this site advocates and defines force.

http://www.as.wvu.edu/~sbb/comm221/chapters/rf.htm

> Steve Booth-Butterfield, professor of Persuasion Theory and Research, boils the Reinforcement Theory down to one main point: consequences influence behavior.

http://spartan.ac.brocku.ca/~lward/Dewey/DEWEY_06.HTML

> Sponsored by the Mead Project, this site posts John Dewey's 1894 essay entitled "The Ego as Cause."

http://www.as.wvu.edu/~sbb/comm221/chapters/inocul.htm

> Steve Booth-Butterfield, professor of Persuasion Theory and Research, explains the Inoculation Theory as it relates to persuasion: present a weak attack on attitudes and beliefs to make them stronger.

Exercise 11.1   Name _____

Whatever You Say

Purpose: To increase your awareness of differing cultural views concerning conflict.

Instructions:

A. Conduct your own survey of the role that culture plays in situations in which the needs or ideas of one person are perceived to be at odds with or in opposition to the needs or ideas of another.

B. Identify 5 people on campus and in your community from different cultures and ask them to complete the questionnaire below.

C. Discuss your findings with a partner.

CONFLICT QUESTIONNAIRE

Give the following definitions to individuals <u>before</u> they answer Question #4:

Withdraw - remove yourself from the conflict

Accommodate - satisfy the needs of the other and neglect your own

Force - satisfy your own needs or advance your own ideas

Compromise - provide some satisfaction for both parties

Collaborate - try to fully address the needs and issues of each party and arrive at a
mutually satisfying solution

	#1	#2	#3	#4	#5
1. What is your cultural origin?					
2. How often do you express opposition to the ideas of another? Never – Seldom – Sometimes – Often – Very Often					
3. How appropriate do you believe it is to express opposition to the ideas of another? Never – Seldom – Sometimes – Often – Very Often					
4. How do you respond when someone expresses opposition to your ideas? Withdraw – Accommodate – Force – Compromise – Collaborate					
Why?					

Exercise 11.2   Name _____

Your Breath Stinks!

Purpose: To examine different styles of conflict management in an effort to become more adept at choosing the most appropriate response.

Instructions:

A. Read the scenarios below.

B. Decide which conflict management style is most appropriate and use it.
   1. Withdrawal. Remove yourself from the conflict.
   2. Accommodate. Satisfy the needs of the other and neglect your own.
   3. Force. Satisfy your own needs or advance your own ideas.
   4. Compromise. Provide some satisfaction for both parties.
   5. Collaborate. Try to fully address the needs and issues of each party and arrive at a mutually satisfying solution.

C. Discuss with a partner which style you chose and why.

Scenario #1: The person seated next to you in class turns to you and says, "Wow, does your breath stink!"

Response:

Scenario #2: You gave your friend money to buy two tickets to a concert: one for you and one for her. You were treating. She says, "I was only able to get one ticket. Sorry. Here's the money for your ticket."

Response:

Exercise 11.3

Name _____

There's One Ticket Left. Who Wants It?

Purpose: To increase your ability to arrive at mutually satisfying solutions through collaboration.

Instructions:
A. Read the following scenarios.
B. Choose one.
C. Attempt to arrive at a mutually satisfying solution that addresses the needs and issues of each party.
D. Write out the conversation.
E. Try out your conversation with a partner. Does your partner find the solution "satisfying"?

Scenario #1: Elian promised to take Ariane to the concert tonight. She has been looking forward to the concert for weeks. Elian was supposed to be done with work by 6:00. His boss told him that he needed him to work overtime until at least 10:00. Elian is about to call Ariane to explain the situation.

Phone Conversation:

Scenario #2: Jennifer and Pam are dying to go to the Rose Bowl with their three roommates. The roommates bought their tickets on the first day that tickets went on sale.   By the time Jennifer and Pam scraped together enough money to buy the tickets, they were sold out. Then one of the roommates decided she wasn't going and told Pam and Jennifer that they could decide who got the ticket.

Conversation:

Exercise 11.4

Name _____

You Are a Slob

Purpose: To improve your ability to de-escalate pseudoconflicts and ego conflicts.

Instructions:

A. In pairs, "deal with" pseudoconflicts #1, #2, and #3 listed below. Through roleplaying, attempt to de-escalate the pseudoconflict before it turns into a real conflict.
B. Discuss with your partner the effectiveness of your tactics.
C. In pairs, "deal with" ego conflicts #4, #5, and #6 listed below. Through roleplaying, attempt to de-escalate the ego conflict to a content level conflict.
D. Discuss with your partner the effectiveness of your tactics.

Scenarios:

1. Your roommate always says that he/she will do the dishes but never does. You wind up doing them. You are starting to harbor resentment toward your roommate.

2. You raise your hand in class, but the instructor never calls on you. You are starting to think that he/she doesn't like you. You're wondering if you should drop the class.

3. You've asked your friend to do something three times in the past week, but he/she is always "too busy" studying. You're starting to feel like your friend is intentionally avoiding you. You are hurt and ready to stop extending invitations.

4. (One roommate to the other when roommate enters apartment one hour too late to go to the movie that both had planned to see together) "Where have you been? You said you'd be home in time to go to the early show. I should have known better than to trust you!"

5. (One roommate to the other) "I'm tired of picking up after you, and I'm tired of you treating me like dirt!"

6. (One roommate to the other) "You've been ripping me off all semester on your share of the phone bill. What kind of an idiot do you take me for?"

Exercise 11.5   Name _____

I'd Die Before I Ate Pizza With You Again

Purpose: To become more adept at recognizing and resolving pseudoconflicts.

Instructions:

A. Identify two "pseudoconflicts" that you've experienced: one that was resolved and one that remains unresolved, just waiting to turn into a real conflict. Remember that a pseudoconflict is not a real conflict. It occurs when a partner believes that desired results cannot be achieved simultaneously when they really can. For example: About twenty years ago, my children decided that they never wanted to go to my husband's favorite Italian restaurant because they hated pizza. My husband decided that he would never take our ungrateful children to his favorite Italian restaurant again because they hated the pizza that he loved. Resolution of pseudoconflict? I suggested that we order a small pizza for us and burgers for the kids. (Duh!)

B. In the designated space below, identify the person who played an instrumental role in resolving the pseudoconflict and explain how their efforts brought about successful results.

C. With a partner, brainstorm a plan to resolve your unresolved pseudoconflict.

D. Try out your plan.

E. With the same partner, discuss the success or lack of success of your plan.

---

1. **RESOLVED PSEUDOCONFLICT:**
   Who played an instrumental role in resolving the situation?
   What specifically did he/she do?

2. **UNRESOLVED PSEUDOCONFLICT:**
   List of things I can do to try to resolve this pseudoconflict:

Exercise 11.6   Name _____

I'll Tell You Who's Lousy With Money, and It Isn't Me

Purpose: To alert and reject the badgering strategies used by partners to goad you into a fight.

Instructions:

A. Identify the badgering or taunting behavior of a friend or loved one, behavior that inevitably ends up in a fight. For example: I know a man (my ex-husband) who used to taunt a certain lovely woman (me) the moment our Mastercard bill arrived. Before I opened the envelope he would ask, "How much did you spend this month?" I would respond, "If you'd deposit your check, I wouldn't have to use the credit card!" The routine was the same. The taunting behavior almost always escalated into a fight.

B. With a partner, brainstorm a list of ways that you could respond to the taunting behavior that would diffuse the taunting rather than escalate it into a full-blown conflict. For example: "Terry, when you ask me how much I've spent this month, I become defensive. I feel that you are really saying that I'm bad with money. I don't want to fight with you, Terry. Let's talk. What's really bothering you?"

C. The next time your friend or loved one begins to badger you, be ready. Try some of the ideas from your list and see which ones work. Good luck!

BADGERING: (explain)

IDEAS TO END BADGERING: (Remember, these are ideas that will alleviate the tension rather than escalate it further.)

SELF EXAMINATION – CHAPTER 11

True/False   If false, explain what is wrong with the statement.

___1. Forcing is a form of conflict management in which people attempt to satisfy their own needs or advance their own ideas.

_____

___2. Withdrawal is appropriate when neither relationship nor issue is really important.

_____

___3. Withdrawal is a form of conflict management in which people attempt to satisfy others' needs while neglecting their own.

_____

___4. Policy conflicts occur when the people involved view "winning" as central to maintaining their positive self-image.

_____

___5. A pseudoconflict is real.

_____

Multiple Choice

___6. Which of the following is NOT true about compromising?
   A.   Both parties give up part of what they really want.
   B.   From a personal-satisfaction standpoint, compromise is win/win.
   C.   Compromising is appropriate when the issue is moderately important.
   D.   Compromising is appropriate when attempts at forcing or collaborating haven't worked.

___7. Which of the following conflict management styles do Verderber and Verderber term the "easiest" way to deal with conflict?
   A. accommodating   B. withdrawal   C. compromising   D. collaborating

___8. When people see "winning" or "losing" as central to maintaining positive self-image, which of the following conflicts is most likely to occur?
   A. ego conflict   B. value conflict   C. policy conflict   D. fact conflict

___9. Which of the following is NOT an affirming nonverbal?
   A.   loud voice   C.   close proximity
   B.   wide eyes   D.   relaxed body posture

___10. Which of the following best describes collaborating?
    A.   a form of conflict management in which people attempt to resolve their conflict by providing at least some satisfaction for both parties
    B.   a form of conflict management that requires some assertiveness and some cooperation
    C.   a form of conflict management that requires both parties to work together to gain resolution
    D.   a form of conflict management in which people attempt to satisfy others' needs while neglecting their own

Complete the Thought

11.   Recognizing and stating ownership of the apparent problem is the first guideline to follow when _____.

12.   A frown or blank facial expression may serve to escalate conflict. These behaviors are referred to as _____.

Essay Questions

13.   Six basic skills should be employed when responding effectively to conflict. Apply and label those basic skills as you respond to the following: "I don't ever want to see you again! Is that clear?"

14.   Six basic guidelines should be followed when initiating conflict. Apply and label those basic guidelines as you address the following scenario: you are upset that your brother/sister borrows your clothes without asking and returns them in shabby condition.

Interpersonal Problem Solver

We've all met her. She might even be your mother: a woman so intent upon tending to the needs of her children that she neglects her own wants and needs; a woman who has time to do her children's washing and ironing, pick up after them, drive them to sporting activities, yet a woman who can't find time to read a book, go to the doctor, or get a good night's sleep. Based upon your understanding of the five styles of conflict management, explain what might be going on in her life. If this woman happens to be your mom, what do you plan to say to her?

Chapter 12: Communicating in Intimate Relationships: Friends, Spouses, and Family

Interactive Chapter Outline

I.   Intimate relationships have identifiable characteristics.

   A.   Warmth/affection is the first, if not the most important, characteristic of intimacy.

   B.   Trust, placing confidence in another in a way that almost always involves some risk, is an important characteristic of intimacy. Four key issues underlie the development of trust.
      1.   Dependable. A dependable partner can be relied upon at all times under all circumstances.
      2.   Responsive. A responsive partner's actions are geared toward the other person's needs.
      3.   Effective conflict-resolver. This partner manages conflicts in a collaborative way.
      4.   Faithful. This partner is secure in the belief that the other person is trustworthy and that the relationship will endure.

   Are you presently involved in an intimate relationship? How important is it to trust your intimate other?

   _____

   _____

   C.   High levels of self-disclosure. Through sharing feelings, partners come to know and understand each other. Even intimate relationships set limits to self-disclosure.

   D.   Commitment. Intimate relationships are characterized by the extent to which a person gives up other relationships in order to devote more time and energy to the primary relationship.

   E.   Formalized through symbols and rituals. Intimates exchange tokens and celebrate events.

   If you are presently involved in an intimate relationship, which of the five characteristics is the most important to you? Least important? Why?

_____

_____

_____

II.   Male-male intimate friendships share common characteristics.

    A.   Male-male intimate behavior is marked by practical help, mutual assistance, and companionship.

    B.   Male-male conversations tend to revolve around sports, sex, work, and vehicles.

    C.   Men talk to same sex friends about women, the news, music, art, and sports.

    D.   Few men discuss relational and personal issues with each other.

    E.   The primary nature of male friendships is to fill roles.

    If you are male, what topics do you talk about with male friends? What topics do you talk about with female friends? Are there topics you avoid with males? females? Why?

_____

_____

_____

III.   Female-female intimate friendships share common characteristics.

    A.   Women's conversation tends to be topical, relational and personal, with the focus on relational and personal.

    B.   Women talk about men, food, relationship problems, family, and fashion.

    C.   Women's friendships develop more quickly than men's and tend to be more intense.

    D.   The tendency to experience the troubles of those close to them and this emotional involvement take a toll, leading to health costs and over-dependence on the relationships.

    If you are female, what topics do you talk about with female friends? with male friends? Are there topics you avoid with males? Females? Why?

_____

_____

_____

_____

IV.   Men and women have different views of intimacy.

   A.   Men view intimacy in relation to physical nearness. Intimacy is defined as practical help, mutual assistance, and companionship.

   B.   Women base intimacy on talking and affection, whether with male or female friends. Intimacy is defined as sharing information, feelings, secrets, and insights.

   C.   Both men and women define intimacy with the same words: *warmth, disclosure of personal feelings,* and *shared activity.*

   D.   Men emphasize or enact actions, warmth, and shared activities.

   E.   Women emphasize or enact warmth and verbal disclosure of personal feelings. With more emphasis on verbal disclosure than action, fun, and companionship, women's friendships are labeled "non-instrumental." With the emphasis of men on activity, their friendships are labeled "instrumental."

         Do you disclose personal feelings more often with male friends or female friends? Why?

         _____

         _____

V.   Male-female friendships can be frustrating.

   A.   Whether sexual or non-sexual, male-female friendships are frustrated by the fact that men and women seek intimacy in different ways.

   B.   Men and women alike have difficulty distinguishing between satisfying intimate friendship relationships and romantic, sexual relationships.

   C.   Romance and sex get in the way of good male-female relationships. Friendship is often diminished by romance and sex. Sex is often capricious. We need to know we can count on a friend.

         Do you have a best friend of the opposite sex? How hard is it to separate friendship from sex? Do you? Why/Why not?

         _____

         _____

VI.   There are three different types of enduring relationships. None is necessarily better than the other.

    A.   Traditional marriage partners share traditional ideology but maintain some independence.
        1.   More emphasis on stability than spontaneity.
        2.   Traditional customs are valued.
        3.   Partners are highly interdependent.
        4.   They engage in conflict rather than avoid it.

    B.   Independent marriage partners share an ideology that embraces change and uncertainty.
        1.   They are interdependent.
        2.   Partners engage in conflict to resolve differences.
        3.   Partners maintain separate physical spaces.
        4.   Partners have difficulty maintaining a daily schedule.

    C.   Separate marriage partners are characterized by a shared traditional ideology but less emotional sharing and less interdependence.
        1.   Conventional in marital and family issues but stress individual freedom.
        2.   Less companionship than traditional or independent marriages.
        3.   Keep a regular daily schedule.

        I would label my marriage as "separate." My ex-husband and I had separate interests and very different careers but always came together on family issues. Consider the marriage of your parents or grandparents or best friends or your own if applicable. Would you label the marriage traditional, independent, or separate? Explain. If you could choose, what type of marriage would you like to have? Why?

        _____

        _____

        _____

VII.   Long-term marriages have three common characteristics.

    A.   Mutual respect. Partners treat each other with dignity, valuing each other for who they are.

    B.   Comfortable level of closeness. Both partners continue to know each other by spending an appropriate amount of time together, in patterned routines.

    C.   Presence of a plan or life vision. Both partners agree on their long-term goals using words like *we* and *us*.

VIII.   The definitions of *family* vary.

A.   Family is a network of people who share their lives over long periods of time bound by ties of marriage, blood, or commitment (legal or otherwise); who consider themselves as a family; and who share a significant history and anticipated future of functioning in a family relationship. (Galvin and Brommel)

B.   Family is a multigenerational social system consisting of at least two interdependent people bound together by a common living space (at one time or another) and a common history, who share some degree of emotional attachment or involvement with one another. (Buerkel-Rothfuss)

C.   Family is a system (network) of individuals who have ongoing relationships with one another, relationships that have existed for some time and are expected to continue to exist.

As you examine your own unique family situation, what is your own unique definition of family?

_____

_____

IX.   Family communication is vital.

A.   Family communication contributes to self-concept formation.
1.   One major responsibility of family members is to talk in ways that will contribute to the development of strong self-concepts in all family members.

What kind of talk went on in your family? Did it contribute to a strong self-concept? Why/Why not?

_____

_____

2.   Praise, acceptance and support, and statements of love enhance self-concept.

When you did something worthy of praise, were family members eager to praise? Why/Why not? Did the praise you did/did not receive affect your self-concept? Explain.

_____

_____

3.   Mixed messages, those in which the verbal and the nonverbal messages are in conflict, diminish self-concept.

Did someone in your family send out mixed messages? Explain.

_____

_____

B.   Family communication supplies recognition and support.
       1.   Recognition and support help family members feel important and help them face and get over difficult times.

             Identify a time when a family member helped you make it through a difficult situation. What did he/she do?

             _____

             _____

             _____

       2.   When people can't get recognition and support from within the family, they go outside for it.

             Have you had to go outside your family for recognition? Why?

             _____

             _____

C.   Family communication establishes models of communication behavior.
       1.   Parents serve as models whether they want to or not.

             What communication has your family modeled that they might regret?

             _____

             _____

       2.   Parents socialize children by teaching them how to manage conflict. My mother used to shake her head and say, "Mary, what you did disappoints me." She never raised her voice.

             How have your parents taught you to manage conflict?

             _____

             _____

X.   Family members can improve their communication.

      A.   Open lines of communication.
             1.   Set up a time to communicate, get together, and talk. Our family spent an hour every evening at the dinner table. If someone had track or basketball or football, then we changed the dinner time, but we never skipped a family dinner.

Did your family have a special time to talk? If yes, when?

_____

2. Establish a pattern of communication for family members to follow in interacting with one another. Ideally, that pattern allows each member to talk with every other member on an equal status level.

Describe the most "unusual" communication pattern you have observed.

_____

_____

B. Confront the effects of power imbalances.
1. Imbalances in referent power occur between two children when one of the children will go to almost any lengths to please the other child.

Describe the balance of power among your brothers and sisters or the brothers and sisters of a friend.

_____

_____

2. If older siblings abuse the power relationship, younger siblings may withdraw or become hostile.

Did you or a sibling find yourselves withdrawing? Explain.

_____

_____

3. Keep lines of communication open so children are free to question why rules for siblings vary. My son is two years older than my daughter. His curfew in high school was one hour later than his sister's. Kelly always used to say, "It isn't fair. I'm just as responsible as Ryan is!"

Did rules for siblings vary in your family? Did you feel comfortable questioning those rules? Why/Why not?

_____

_____

C. Recognize and adapt to change.
1. Family members are often the last to realize that family members change and need to practice the skill of perception checking.
2. Family members need to be alert to changes that indicate stress or emotional distress. When my son went away to college, his words said

that all was well. His flat, tight voice told me there were problems. Have you witnessed signs of distress among your siblings?

3. Family members need to use empathy to ensure equitable family relations. If something in your family seems inequitable is your family willing to talk about it?

4. Respect individual interests.
   a. Family communication is often marked by indifference or apathy.
   b. Recognize what one person thinks is important.

Does your family ask for your opinion? On what issues? How does it make you feel?

_____

_____

D. Manage conflicts equitably.

1. Develop rules for how differences between members will be handled.

Some families avoid conversing about subjects on which there is likely to be disagreement. Was there a forbidden topic in your family?

2. Some families hold meetings and work out the problem jointly with neutral members serving as mediators. Conflict is viewed as a way to promote a win/win outcome.

Do you come from a family of mediators? Were you ever the "focus" of a family meeting? Explain. Did it help?

_____

_____

3. Some families use coercive or forcing behaviors.
   a. Conflict ends with the weakest acceding to the wishes of the most powerful.

Among siblings, describe your role. Were you the most powerful? Least powerful? Somewhere in the middle?

_____

_____

   b. When force is met by resistance, family violence may result.
   c. Physical abuse is most often perpetrated by men.
   d. Both men and women engage in verbal abuse.
   e. Verbal abusers are likely to lack appropriate communication skills, including those related to constructive conflict management.

Is there a family member who always resorts to coercive or forceful behavior to win an argument? How do you respond to that person?

_____

_____

XI.   Problems in intimate relationships result from verbal jealousy and sex-role stereotyping.

A.   Jealousy, the suspicion of rivalry or unfaithfulness, is one of the major destructive forces in relationships.
1.   Low self-esteem triggers jealousy.
2.   Women are more threatened by lack of attention and separateness.
3.   Men are more threatened by positive attentions to another person.
4.   The answer to reducing jealousy is to raise the level of trust.

Have you been involved in an intimate relationship in which the partner expressed jealousy? Explain. Were you both able to reduce the suspicious behavior by addressing trust? Explain.

_____

_____

B.   Sex-role stereotyping continues to be a problem in intimate relationships.
1.   Men need to develop more nurturing skills.
2.   Women need to develop skills that enable them to present their own point of view clearly and firmly.

Describe the sex-role stereotyping, if any, that you observe in your parents or the parents of a friend.

_____

_____

XII.   Male-female relationships can be improved.

A.   Male-female relationships can be improved if partners acknowledge the effects of their early conditioning on their interpersonal communication.

B.   Male-female relationships can improve if men and women examine the dependency relationships that result from sex-role stereotypes.
1.   The climate for equality in communication between men and women is difficult to establish in a society that values masculine behavior more highly than feminine behavior.

In your family, are masculine behaviors valued more highly than feminine behaviors? Explain.

_____

_____

2. Women jeopardize their relationships with other women to advance more socially desirable relationships with men. Men don't risk same-sex friendships in this way because masculine behavior is more valued.

Have you cancelled an evening with a friend of the same-sex to do something at the last minute with someone of the opposite sex? Why?

_____

_____

3. Male-female relationships can improve if men and women monitor sex-role-based tendencies toward communication dominance or passivity. A good communication climate results in part from equality.

Describe a male-female relationship in which you are presently engaged. Is the male more dominant and the female more passive, or do both partners work for equality in the relationship? Explain.

_____

_____

_____

Key Terms in Chapter 12
(Define each of the terms below.)

comfortable level of closeness _____

_____

dependable partner _____

_____

effective conflict-resolving partner _____

_____

faithful partner _____

_____

family _____

_____

independent marriage partners _____

_____

intimate friends _____

_____

intimate relationships _____

_____

jealousy _____

_____

life vision _____

_____

mutual respect _____

_____

power imbalances _____

_____

responsive partner _____

_____

separate marriage partners _____

_____

sex-role stereotyping _____

_____

traditional marriage partners _____

_____

trust _____

_____

Interesting Sites on the Internet

http://www.awc.cc.az.us/psy/dgershaw/lol/Marriages.Last.htm
> Adapted from the work of psychologists Jeanette and Robert Lauer, this work by David Gershaw examines seven reasons why partners believe their relationships have endured.

http://www.bestyears.com/marriagelast.html
> Author Mike Bellah discusses the affect of midlife crises on marriages and how midlife marriage partners can work to sustain their marriage.

http://www.geocities.com/lilacbiru/creatingstrongsatisfyingmarrigae.html
> This site explores creating a strong and satisfying marriage and examines managing conflicts and strengthening the relationship.

http://www.etsu.edu/philos/faculty/hugh/honesty.htm
> Authors Graham and LaFollette, in an article found in the *Journal of Social and Personal Relationships*, explore the role that honesty plays in developing and sustaining intimate relationships.

http://www.healthandage.com/Home/gid2=1284
> Presented by the Novartis Foundation for Gerontology, this site contains a discussion by Andra Stanton (Clinical Social Worker, U-Mass) of gender differences present in conversations and steps to take to avoid misunderstandings.

Exercise 12.1   Name _____

I Love the Way She Swings a Bat

Purpose: To better understand what men and women value in intimate relationships.

Instructions:
A. Ask five men and five women to complete the questionnaire below.
B. Together with a partner, compare your findings.
C. Identify the most important and least important quality cited by men to describe intimate relationships.
D. Identify the most important and least important quality cited by women to describe an intimate relationship.
E. Do your findings support the findings cited by Verderber and Verderber, that men emphasize shared activities, women emphasize verbal disclosure of personal feelings, and both men and women emphasize warmth?

INTIMACY QUESTIONNAIRE

I.   What one quality is most important TO YOU in an intimate male/female relationship?
    A.   Warmth
    B.   Verbal disclosure of personal feelings
    C.   Activities that you both do together

2.   What one quality is least important TO YOU in an intimate male/female relationship?
    A.   Warmth
    B.   Verbal disclosure of personal feelings
    C.   Activities that you both do together

Male #1	Male #2	Male #3	Male #4	Male #5
1.	1.	1.	1.	1.
2.	2.	2.	2.	2.
Female #1	Female #2	Female #3	Female #4	Female #5
1.	1.	1.	1.	1.
2.	2.	2.	2.	2.

Exercise 12.2   Name _____

He Wants Snow and She Wants Sun

Purpose: To gain greater insight into the common characteristics of long-term marriages.

Instructions:

A. Identify a couple who has been married for at least twenty-five years.

B. Ask the couple to complete the questionnaire below.

C. Verderber and Verderber cite three common characteristics of long-term marriages that include mutual respect, a comfortable level of closeness, and presence of a plan or life vision. Discuss with the class whether your findings support those cited by the authors.

MARRIAGE QUESTIONNAIRE

I.   **Mutual Respect**

    A.   Do you feel that your partner and you treat each other with dignity? Explain:

    B.   Do you feel that your partner and you value each other for what you are? Explain:

2.   **Comfortable Level of Closeness**

    A.   Do you feel that your partner and you spend an appropriate amount of time together? Explain:

    B.   Do your partner and you have activities that you typically do together regularly? Explain:

3.   **Presence of a Life Vision**

    A.   Do your partner and you agree on a long-term goal? Explain:

    B.   Do your partner and you speak of plans for the future using words like *we* and *us*? Explain:

Exercise 12.3   Name _____

How About Those Packers!

Purpose: To become better acquainted with differences that exist in male-male intimate conversations and female-female intimate conversations.

Instructions:
A. Identify three males and three females to respond to the following questionnaire.
B. Verderber and Verderber cite the following as common characteristics of intimate female-female friendships: conversations focus on relationships and personal issues. Are your findings supportive?
C. Verderber and Verderber cite the following as common characteristics of intimate male-male friendships: conversations focus on sports, sex, work, and vehicles. Are your findings supportive?
D. Discuss your findings with students in class.

CONVERSATION QUESTIONNAIRE

1.   When you are speaking to your best same-sex friend, what subject do you most enjoy talking about?

2.   When you are speaking to your best same-sex friend, what subject do you least enjoy talking about?

Male #1	Male #2	Male #3
1.	1.	1.
2.	2.	2.

Female #1	Female #2	Female #3
1.	1.	1.
2.	2.	2.

Exercise 12.4   Name _____

Que Vous Etes Belle!

Purpose: To better understand what we do to create friendships.

Instructions:
A. Verderber and Verderber cite the following as characteristics of an intimate relationship: warmth/affection, trust, high levels of self-disclosure, commitment, and formalized rituals. Using these characteristics, identify one person whom you consider to be an intimate friend (sexual or non-sexual).
B. Antoine de Saint Exupéry writes in his book, *The Little Prince*, that to have a friend one must *creér des liens* (create bonds). He also writes that one must be *utile* (useful). Using Exupéry's criteria for friendship, respond to the survey questions.
C. Discuss your answers with students in class.

FRIENDSHIP SURVEY

1.   What do you think is the most important thing that you have done for your friend which created a "bond" of friendship?

2.   What do you think is the most important thing that your friend has done for you which created a "bond" of friendship?

3.   Create a list of "things you do" to be useful to your friend.

Exercise 12.5

Name _____

I Trust You, I Think

Purpose: To better understand how our own actions affect the trust we have in intimate partners.

Instructions:

A. Authors Gold, Ryckman, and Lenney, in *The Journal of Social Psychology,* identify three characteristics in a partner that cultivate trust: predictability, dependability, and faith. With a partner, discuss the role that each of these characteristics plays in your "trust" relationships.

B. Identify your most intimate "opposite sex" or "same sex" partner. Complete the questionnaire and discuss your answers with a partner.

TRUST QUESTIONNAIRE

1	2	3	4	5	6	7	8	9	10
Not At All				Somewhat					Very Much

Evaluate your "trust" in your intimate other using the above scale.

RATING

1. PREDICTABLE
    (a) How predictable is your partner?   (a) _____
    (b) Does he/she fulfill promises and act positively?   (b) _____
2. DEPENDABLE
    (c) How dependable is your partner?   (c) _____
3. FAITHFUL
    (d) Do you have a sense of security about
         the future of the relationship?   (d) _____
4. COMMUNALLY ORIENTED
    (e) Do you focus more on your partner's needs
         than on whether your partner is doing his/her   (e) _____
         fair share (mutual exchange)?
5. TRUST WORTHY
    (f) How much do you trust your partner?   (f) _____

Exercise 12.6   Name _____

Wow, Have You Chunked Up in College!

Purpose: To enhance your awareness of the communication that occurs within your family and the role that this communication plays in shaping your self-concept.

Instructions:

A. At your next family gathering, use the chart below to evaluate the communication that takes place between you and family members.

B. Each time a family member expresses praise, acceptance, or love, record it.

C. Each time a family member expresses insults, lack of acceptance, or hate, record it.

D. Discuss the results of this exercise with your family members. For example: "Mom, do you realize that you have insulted my choices three times in this conversation? What's going on?" or "Dad, it means a lot to me when you repeatedly express your acceptance of my decisions. Thanks."

AFFIRMING COMMUNICATION		
Praise	**Acceptance**	**Love**
Mother			
Father			
Sibling #1			
Sibling #2			

UNAFFIRMING COMMUNICATION		
Insult	**Lack of Acceptance**	**Hate**
Mother			
Father			
Sibling #1			
Sibling #2			

SELF EXAMINATION – CHAPTER 12

True/False
If false, explain what is wrong with the statement.

___1. Both men and women define intimacy with the same words: *warmth, disclosure of personal feelings,* and *shared activity.*

___2. Traditional marriage partners engage in conflict rather than avoid it.

___3. Men's friendships develop more quickly than women's.

___4. In intimate relationships, partners do not set limits to self-disclosure.

___5. The conversation of men tends to be topical, relational, and personal, with the focus on relational and personal.

Multiple Choice

___6. Which of the following is NOT a common characteristic of a long-term marriage?
   A.   fidelity
   B.   life vision
   C.   mutual respect
   D.   comfortable level of closeness

___7. Which of the following is most likely to trigger jealousy in both men and women?
   A.   lack of attention
   B.   separateness
   C.   positive attention to another
   D.   low self-esteem

___8. Male-male intimate behavior is marked by which of the following?
   A.   practical help, companionship, relational issues
   B.   companionship, relational issues, personal issues
   C.   practical help, companionship, mutual assistance
   D.   practical help, relational issues, mutual assistance

___9. Which of the following characteristics best describes an independent marriage?
   A.   more emphasis on stability than spontaneity; engage in conflict rather than avoid it
   B.   engage in conflict to resolve differences; maintain separate physical spaces
   C.   keep a regular daily schedule; stress individual freedom
   D.   engage in conflict to resolve differences; partners are highly interdependent

___10. Which of the following definitions most inclusively defines *family*, as we know it today?
   A.   a network of people who share their lives over long periods bound by marriage
   B.   a multigenerational social system consisting of at least two interdependent people bound by common living space
   C.   a system of individuals with an ongoing relationship that has existed for some time and will continue to exist
   D.   none of the above

Complete the Thought

11.   A system of individuals who have ongoing relationships with one another, relationships that have existed for some time and are expected to continue to exist, is known as

   _____ .

12.   Jealousy, one of the major destructive forces in relationships, is triggered by

   _____ .

Essay Questions

13.   Verderber and Verderber cite three characteristics of a "long-term" marriage. Identify one long-term marriage with which you are familiar and talk about it in light of those three characteristics.

14.   Verderber and Verderber identify three reasons why strong family communication is vital. Identify and explain each reason.

Interpersonal Problem Solver

Your friend is in love. He displays all of the characteristics of someone involved in an intimate relationship. The young woman, on the other hand, doesn't. Applying what you know about the identifiable characteristics of intimate relationships, explain what you see in him that you don't see in her. Should you tell him?

Chapter 13: Communicating in the Workplace

Interactive Chapter Outline

I.   Two documents help to "advertise you for interviews."

        A.   The cover letter, expressing your interest in a position, follows specific guidelines.

            1.   The letter is addressed to the person with the authority to hire.

            2.   The letter answers the following questions:

                a.   Where and how did you find out about the position?

                b.   What is your reason for being interested in the company?

                c.   What are your key skills and accomplishments?

                d.   How do you fit the job requirements?

                e.   What items of special interest support your potential for the job?

                f.   Did you request an interview?

            If an employer has too many applications, he/she may discard applicants based upon the cover letter. Have you ever written a cover letter? Did it follow the guidelines cited above? Do you think the letter helped you get the job?

        B.   The resume, a summary of your skills and accomplishments, includes the following ten pieces of information:

            1.   Name, address, and phone number where you can be reached.

            2.   One-sentence statement of job objective focusing on your expertise.

            3.   Employment history, paid and unpaid, dates and duties.

            4.   Education with focus on courses related to job.

            5.   Military experience.

            6.   Relevant professional certifications and affiliations.

            7.   Community activities, offices held and dates.

            8.   Special skills.

            9.   Interests and activities related to your objective.

            10.   A statement that references are available upon request. Make sure you have permission of the people you intend to use as references.

            Have you ever written a resume? Did you like the end result? Did you refrain from "stretching the truth?" Was it under three typewritten pages?

II.   Guidelines help you to prepare for an interview.

        A.   Do your homework by learning as much as possible about the company.

        B.   Rehearse anticipated questions and answers aloud.

C. Dress conservatively.

D. Arrive promptly.

E. Be alert, look at the interviewer, and listen actively.

F. Give yourself time to think before answering.
   1. If you hadn't anticipated a question, give yourself time.
   2. If you don't understand a question, ask interviewer to paraphrase it.

G. Ask questions about the type of work you will be doing.

H. Show enthusiasm for the job.

I. Do not engage in long discussions of salary.

J. Do not harp on benefits.

I wore a bright yellow, short dress to my interview for the job I presently have. As far as I can remember, conservative clothing is the only guideline I ignored. My daughter wore a gray business suit to her final interview for a position as a Madison police officer. She was told she didn't get the job because she was "too young." (She was twenty-two but looked sixteen.) Have you ignored any of the guidelines? Did you get the job?

III. Interview questions come in different forms.

A. Open questions are broad-based, allowing the interviewee to respond with whatever information he/she wishes.
   1. Open questions take time to answer.
   2. The respondent has more control.

A typical question that I ask candidates when I serve on the appointment committee is, "What would you like us to know about you that you haven't already had an opportunity to say?" Ask another open question.

_____

B. Closed questions are narrow-focused, requiring very brief answers.
   1. Closed questions allow the interviewer to obtain large amounts of information in a short time.
   2. The interviewer has more control.

"What was your major?" Ask another closed question.

_____

C.   Neutral questions allow a person to give an answer without direction from the interviewer. "Why are you applying for this job?" Ask another.

_____

D.   Leading questions suggest the interviewer's preference. "Would you be willing to put in a twelve-hour day?" Ask another leading question.

_____

E.   Primary questions are planned ahead of time by the interviewer.

F.   Secondary questions are either planned or spontaneous and pursue an answer to a primary question in order to motivate the person to enlarge upon an answer.

During my daughter's recent interview with the Madison Police Department, the chief asked four open questions with no secondary questions. During your most recent interview, were most of the questions open or closed? Did the interviewer use secondary questions? Were the questions ones you had anticipated? Are you about to interview for a job? If yes, make a list of the questions you think they will ask.

_____

_____

_____

IV.   The person conducting the interview follows a set procedure.

A.   Open the interview by stating the purpose of the interview and giving your name.

B.   Ask the interview questions.

C.   Explain to the interviewee what will happen next.

D.   Close the interview in a courteous yet neutral way.

Did your most recent interview follow the preceding procedure? How well do you feel the interviewer did?

V.   Careful attention to communication creates an effective working relationship between supervisors and subordinates.

A.   Supervisors have specific communication responsibilities.
    1.   They must instruct subordinates, using clear, vivid language.

233

2. They must give job performance feedback offering constructive criticism.

3. They must influence subordinates to meet personal and work goals but must also understand employee needs.

    a. They must be effective listeners.

    b. They must be skilled at paraphrasing and perception checking.

Think about your present supervisor. How would you evaluate his/her communication in the above areas? Where should he/she perform better?

_____

B. Subordinates have specific communication responsibilities.

1. They must listen, question, and paraphrase.

2. They must ask for feedback and assert themselves.

3. They must establish an exchange relationship by asking, "How can I establish a more effective working relationship with my boss?" Then, they communicate that willingness to the boss.

How effectively would you rate your communication as a subordinate? Where do you need to improve? Explain.

_____

_____

VI. How well we get along with co-workers depends upon communication competence.

A. If you are insensitive to needs and feelings of co-workers, you are not likely to find these relationships satisfying.

B. Managed disagreements may lead to more creative and productive solutions to problems.

C. Effective interpersonal communication, including listening, turn-taking, and empathizing, helps to maintain healthy working relationships.

How well do you get along with co-workers? Can you identify one who appears insensitive to the needs of others? Have you found a way to address that insensitivity? Are you someone who shuns disagreements or have you engaged in productive disagreements?

VII. Self-managed work teams produce successful results if communication is strong.

A. Effective communication of high standards for work, and acceptance of these standards by team members, generate productive team pressure.

B.   Self-managed teams share a wealth of job-related information that is crucial to the team if it hopes to be productive.

C.   Self-managed teams tend to have good working relationships causing people to stay with the job.

I teach two "integrated studies" courses with co-workers. In one of the courses, I'm teamed with a gentle, cooperative problem-solver who addresses both issues and feelings. I teach another course with six colleagues: a geographer, an historian, an anthropologist, and three English professors. High standards and information sharing abound, as do "territorial" issues. We have weathered tumultuous times as we attempt to nurture trust. Have you ever been a member of a self-managed work team? How well did you communicate with each other? What problems arose? How well did you handle them? Would you rather work alone or on a team? Why?

_____

_____

_____

VIII.   Individuals with boundary-spanning roles, whose central task is to deal with people outside the organization, need refined communication skills.

A.   Customer service providers need skills like empathizing, listening, responding effectively to conflict, and using equality-oriented language.

B.   Customer service providers have little control over the policies that they must follow. This lack of control should be explained to the customer.
I recently bought a set of Spanish tapes for my daughter. I told the clerk that I wasn't sure that these were the correct tapes. She said nothing. When I returned them the next day, she said: "I'm sorry, I can give you store credit but not cash." Why hadn't she explained that the day before? Have you had a similar incident?

C.   Customer service providers are held responsible for those policies and thus need to explain the reason behind the policy to maintain good communication.
Recently, a customer service provider for a phone company said to me, "The bottom line is there is nothing more I can do for you." Bottom line?

Identify your most frustrating experience with a customer service provider. How might this person have avoided the communication problem?

_____

_____

IX.   Leaders exhibit leadership traits.

    A.   In ability, effective leaders exceed average group members in intelligence, scholarship, insight, and verbal facility.

    B.   In sociability, effective leaders exceed average group members in dependability, activeness, cooperativeness, and popularity.

    C.   In motivation, effective leaders exceed average group members in initiative, persistence, and enthusiasm.

    D.   In communication, effective leaders exceed average group members in most skills discussed in the text.

    Identify a leader whom you truly admire. Does she/he exhibit the traits mentioned? Explain. Identify the "worst" leader you know. Does she/he lack the traits mentioned? Explain. How do you think he/she managed to get the leadership position?

    _____

    _____

    _____

X.   Effective leaders possess skills.

    A.   Task-oriented leaders exercise direct control over people and groups.
        1.   More work gets done with task-oriented leaders.
        2.   Task-oriented leaders may create discontent or stifle creativity.

    B.   Person-oriented leaders suggest ways of proceeding, but encourage group members to determine what will actually be done.
        1.   Less work gets done when no leadership exists.
        2.   Person-oriented leaders are more friendly.

    C.   Success of an individual's leadership style depends upon three questions:
        1.   How good are the leader's interpersonal relations with the group?
        2.   How clearly defined are goals and tasks?
        3.   To what degree does the group accept the leader's legitimate authority?

    In IX, you identified an effective leader. Is she/he more task-oriented or person-oriented or both? Has her/his leadership style caused problems? Explain.

    _____

    _____

XI.   Effective leaders create reality through framing.

A.   Framing is a mental model for managing meaning. It involves the selection and highlighting of some aspects of a subject and the exclusion of others.

B.   Framing asserts that our interpretation should be taken as "real."

C.   Framers use five forms of language:
1.   Metaphors such as "You are survivors."
2.   Jargon or catch phrases such as "We aren't afraid to get our hands dirty."
3.   Contrast allows us to see what a situation is NOT. "This is NOT a way of saying that your hard work will go unnoticed."
4.   Spin frames cast the change in either a positive or negative light. "Our decision to deny keys to all teachers in the district is, in no way, an indication that we fail to respect your integrity."
5.   Story frames make the change seem more "real." "I remember when I was first hired by this company, I . . . ."

D.   Frames continue to be reframed using techniques like personalization. The leader points out specific behaviors that one member needs to adopt in order to be in line with change.

Observe a leader. Give examples of the framing techniques she/he uses in order to gather support. How effective do you believe his/her framing techniques were?

_____

_____

XII. Effective leaders work at being effective.

A.   They are knowledgeable about the particular tasks.

B.   They develop mental models for managing meaning. Framing is one such model.

C.   They work harder than anyone else.

D.   They are personally committed to group goals and needs.

E.   They are willing to be decisive.

F.   They develop people skills as well as task skills.

Describe a leadership role that you have held. Were you effective? Why/Why not? Have you ever refused a leadership role? Why?

_____

_____

XIII. Coaching, the hands-on process of helping others improve their work performance, requires skills.

    A.   An effective coach is a technically adept, keen observer.

    B.   An effective coach analyzes and supplies specific suggestions for improvement.

    C.   An effective coach creates a supportive problem-solving environment.

Have you been coached by someone who made you feel like "trying harder"? My son's JV basketball coach said, "Ryan, you made six mistakes in the game last night. I don't want to see your face again until you can identify the six mistakes." Ryan watched the game video over and over. I could hear him mumbling, "Four, I only see four." Hours later, he found his sixth mistake. He identified the errors to his coach, who then announced that Ryan was being moved up to varsity. Interesting problem-solving approach. Share an "effective coaching" example. Share an "ineffective coaching" example.

_____

_____

XIV. Counselors need to observe rules as they discuss emotional problems with another in order to resolve the problem or help the other cope better.

    A.   Effective counselors assure confidentiality.
        1.   If confidentiality could jeopardize the health or well-being of others, ethical counselors must advise the other person to disclose the information.
        2.   If confidentiality could jeopardize the health or well-being of others, inform him/her that you are ethically bound to disclose the information.

Once, a student came to my office and shut the door. He told me that he had severe mental problems and that his counselor feared that he might kill someone. The student explained that that someone would be ME. Ouch! Perhaps this is an extreme case and perhaps he had come to me less for counseling and more for threatening, but I did explain that I was ethically bound to disclose this information. Have you ever been ethically bound to disclose a confidentiality?

B.   Effective counselors are good listeners.
   1.   Effective counselors ask questions for clarification.
   2.   Effective counselors paraphrase.
   3.   Effective counselors provide comforting replies.

C.   Effective counselors help colleagues find help.

How often do co-workers turn to you for counseling? What qualities do you have that make you an effective/ineffective counselor?

_____

_____

XV.   Effective leaders are adept at managing group problem solving.

A.   Effective leaders set agendas.
   1.   Agendas are given to members in advance of the meeting.
   2.   Problem-solving agendas outline the steps in problem solving.

B.   Effective leaders gatekeep.
   1.   Silent members are drawn into the discussion.
   2.   Overzealous speakers are controlled.

C.   Effective leaders question appropriately.
   1.   Appropriate questions initiate discussion.
   2.   Appropriate questions focus discussion.
   3.   Appropriate questions probe for information.
   4.   Appropriate questions deal with interpersonal problems that develop.

D.   Effective leaders summarize and crystalize consensus.

Think of the last group meeting in which you participated. Did one person dominate the conversation? Did others sit in silence? Were gatekeeping efforts employed to address the issue?

_____

_____

Key Terms in Chapter 13
(Define each of the terms below.)

agenda _____

_____

boundary-spanning role _____

_____

closed question _____

_____

coaching _____

_____

counseling _____

_____

cover letter _____

_____

framing _____

_____

gatekeeping _____

_____

leadership style _____

_____

leading question _____

_____

neutral question _____

_____

open question _____

_____

person-oriented leader _____

_____

primary question _____

_____

resume _____

_____

secondary question _____

_____

task-oriented leader _____

_____

Interesting Sites on the Internet

http://jobstar.org/tools/resume/cletters.cfm
> This site identifies a *good* cover letter and recommends both cover letter resources on the Web and books on cover letters.

http://owl.english.purdue.edu/handouts/pw/p_skilist.html
> This site offers a list of action words that you may want to incorporate into your resume.

http://www.rockportinstitute.com/resumes.html
> Nicholas Lore, in an excerpt from his book *The Pathfinder: How to Choose or Change Your Career for a Lifetime of Satisfaction and Success*, explains how to prepare a successful resume.

http://www.careercc.com/interv3.shtml
> Sponsored by Career Consulting Corner, this site offers interviewing tips including questions to ask and questions to be prepared to answer.

http://www.breakoutofthebox.com/ldrho.htm
> Leadership development coach Mary R. Bast, Ph.D., identifies nine leadership styles and offers advice for the development of skills aimed at reducing problems that accompany each style.

Exercise 13.1   Name _____

Please Hire Me

Purpose: To create an effective cover letter.

Instructions:

A. Describe, in detail, a job that you are seeking for the summer (short term) or after graduation (career position). Use the following questions to assist you in your description of the job.
   1. What details about the company do I need to know, and what qualities are likely to be valued in that company?
   2. What specific job in the company am I seeking, and what qualities are needed in that job?
   3. What details about the specific job for which I am applying mesh well with my abilities and training?

B. Prepare a cover letter, similar to the letter in Chapter 13, which expresses interest in the job that you have described above. Make sure the letter addresses the specific guidelines mentioned below:
   1. Address letter to the person with the authority to hire.
   2. Explain where and how you found out about the position.
   3. Explain your reason for being interested in the company.
   4. Explain your key skills and accomplishments.
   5. Explain how you fit the job requirements.
   6. Highlight some special details that support your potential for the job.
   7. Request an interview.

C. Give your cover letter to a partner and ask him/her to critique it.

D. Revise the cover letter and print it on bond paper.

Exercise 13.2   Name _____

I'll Work for Food

Purpose: To create an impressive resume.

Instructions:

A. Refer to Chapter 13 in order to identify the ten pieces of information that should be included in a resume.

B. Identify a position or internship for which you would like to apply in the near future. (Even if you are not contemplating employment, address this assignment as though you were.)

C. Create a one-page resume using most, if not all, of the following:
   1. Name, address, and phone number where you can be reached.
   2. One-sentence statement of job objective focusing on experience.
   3. Employment history, paid and nonpaid, dates and duties.
   4. Education with focus on courses related to the job.
   5. Military experience.
   6. Relevant professional certifications and affiliations.
   7. Community activities, offices held and dates.
   8. Special skills.
   9. Interests and activities related to your objective.
   10. Statement that references are available upon request. Obtain permission of people whose names you intend to use.

D. Give your resume to a partner and ask him/her to critique it.

E. Revise the resume and print on bond paper.

Exercise 13.3　　　　　　　　　　Name _____

Good Question, but I Don't Know the Answer

Purpose:　　To become more adept at the interview process.

Instructions:
A. Choose a company with which you would like to interview for a position.
B. Decide on the exact position that you want with the company.
C. Assume that your cover letter and resume have been sent to the company and they have notified you that you will have an interview within the next two weeks.
D. Brainstorm the qualities and experience you have that would make you an excellent candidate for that position.
E. Second-guess the interview committee by anticipating six primary questions. Include four open questions which allow you to respond with whatever information you wish. Include two closed questions that are narrow-focused and require very brief answers. Write your questions below.
F. Roleplay with a partner. If you have already created a cover letter and resume for this position, share them with your partner. Give your partner the questions, and have the partner conduct the interview.
G. Partner: During the interview, ask several "secondary questions" which pursue the interviewee's responses to "primary questions."

_____

Open Questions:

1.

2.

3.

4.

Closed Questions:

1.

2.

Exercise 13.4   Name _____

I Quit! / You're Fired!

Purpose: To become more sensitive to communication responsibilities of supervisors and subordinates.

Instructions:

A. Find a partner. Assign one student the role of manager. Assign the other student the role of server.

B. Manager: Rehearse the list of complaints that you have about the server:
   1. Employee sometimes arrives late for work.
   2. Employee leaves at the time it says on the schedule but leaves before tables in his/her section are cleaned.
   3. Employee "barks" at other employees.

C. Server: Rehearse the list of complaints that you have about the manager:
   1. You told the manager when he/she hired you that you had another job and that your hours would have to be arranged around the other job. Now the manager is scheduling hours so that your two jobs overlap.
   2. You feel that the other servers aren't doing their share of the work. You have to yell at them to pay attention to their customers because the manager doesn't seem to notice.

D. Manager and Server: Try to find an acceptable solution to the situation as you roleplay the following scenario:

   Manager explains to server why he/she feels the employee is rude and that if things don't change, manager will have to fire server. Server explains he/she really needs the money but isn't happy with the status quo and is considering leaving.

E. Evaluate your partner's handling of this work-related problem using the rubric on the following page. Manager evaluates employee and employee evaluates manager.

MANAGER GRADING RUBRIC

Excellent	Very Good	Good	Average	Below Average
9-10	8	7	5-6	1-4

_____ I.   Describes work-related problem to employee using clear, vivid language.

_____ 2.   Offers constructive criticism that includes praise.

_____ 3.   Provides proof that he/she understands employee needs.

_____ 4.   Provides evidence of effective listening through paraphrasing and perception checks.

EMPLOYEE GRADING RUBRIC

Excellent	Very Good	Good	Average	Below Average
9-10	8	7	5-6	1-4

_____ 1.   Communicates work problem to employer using clear, vivid language.

_____ 2.   Listens, questions, paraphrases.

_____ 3.   Asks for feedback.

_____ 4.   Assumes joint responsibility for solving the problem.

Exercise 13.5

Name _____

She's the Best Professor on Campus

Purpose: To become more aware of the framing techniques used by effective professors as they attempt to motivate students.

Instructions:

A. Framing is a mental model for managing meaning. It involves the selection and highlighting of some aspects of a subject and the exclusion of others. Familiarize yourself with the 5 forms of language used by framers, language that creates reality.
   1. Metaphors: "Molly, you're the Wonder Woman of this class."
   2. Catch phrases or jargon: "Alex, you really know how to get the discussion ball rolling."
   3. Contrast allows others to see what a situation is NOT: "I'm not saying that our discussion would have failed without you, Mayumi, but you certainly added life to this topic."
   4. Spin frames cast change in either a positive or negative light: "My decision to postpone the exam is to give my precious students more time to prepare for success."
   5. Story frames make the change seem more real: "I remember when the semester began. No one in this class would talk, but now . . ."
B. Select one of your professors whom you believe to be an especially effective leader.
C. During one class session observe his/her leadership in the classroom. Make note of his/her framing language.
D. Using the chart below, record that language.
E. Ask yourself if the mental modeling of the professor was effective or ineffective in motivating students.

PROFESSORIAL REALITY SHAPING	
Metaphors	
Catch phrases	
Contrasting Language	
Spin frames	
Stories	

Exercise 13.6   Name _____

I Swear He Had Eyes in the Back of His Head

Purpose: To identify the qualities that make some coaches effective and others ineffective.

Instructions:
A. Review the following skills that Verderber and Verderber cite as essential for effective "hands-on" coaching: coaching that improves the work performance of athletes.
   1. She/he is a technically adept, keen observer.
   2. She/he analyzes and supplies specific suggestions for improvement.
   3. She/he creates a supportive problem-solving environment.
B. Identify one of your coaches whom you believe to have been the "most skilled." Using the chart below, cite specific examples of his/her effective coaching.
C. Identify one of your coaches whom you believe to have been the "least skilled." Using the chart below, cite specific examples of his/her ineffective coaching.
D. With a partner, discuss the relationship between ineffective coaching and team success. Can a team with an ineffective coach make it to State? Why? Why not?

MOST EFFECTIVE COACH: _____

A. Technically adept, keen observer (example of success):

B. Specific suggestions for improvement (example of success):

C. Supportive problem-solving (example of success):

LEAST EFFECTIVE COACH: _____

A. Technically adept, keen observer (example of how he/she failed):

B. Specific suggestions for improvement (example of how he/she failed):

C. Supportive problem-solving (example of how he/she failed):

SELF EXAMINATION – CHAPTER 13

True/False   **If false, explain what is wrong with the statement.**

___1. Counselors must always assure confidentiality.

_____

___2. Open questions allow the interviewer more control.

_____

___3. Primary questions are spontaneous.

_____

___4. Task-oriented leaders exercise direct control over people.

_____

___5. Weight and height are included in a resume.

_____

Multiple Choice

___6. Which of the following is NOT included in the guidelines for interviewing?
- A. show enthusiasm
- B. dress smartly
- C. do not harp on benefits
- D. do not engage in long discussions of salary

___7. Which of the following is LEAST typical of a self-managed team?
- A. good working relationship and reduced pressure
- B. share a wealth of job-related information and have good working relationship
- C. stay with the job longer
- D. high standards and productive team pressure

___8. Which of the following is the most effective leadership style?
- A. task-oriented
- B. person-oriented
- C. combination of task-oriented and person-oriented
- D. none of the above

___9. Which of the following is NOT included in a cover letter?
- A. where and how you found out about the position
- B. how you fit the job requirements
- C. a one-sentence statement of job objective focusing on your expertise
- D. items of special interest that support your potential for the job

___10. Which of the following most accurately describes a leading question?
    A.   gives respondent more control
    B.   allows respondent freedom to answer
    C.   suggests interviewer's preference
    D.   narrows focus, requiring very brief answers

Complete the Thought

11.   "What would you like us to know about you that you haven't already had an opportunity to say?" is an example of _____.

12.   The selection and highlighting of some aspects of a subject and the exclusion of others in order to manage meaning is known as _____.

Essay Questions

13.   An effective interviewer asks appropriate questions. Assume that you are interviewing applicants for night supervisor at a fast-food restaurant. Define and label six questions that fall into each of the following categories: (a) open, (b) closed, (c) neutral, (d) leading, (e) primary, (f) secondary.

14.   A cover letter addresses answers to six specific questions. Identify those questions.

Interpersonal Problem Solver

Your roommate has an interview for a security job on campus: escorting female students at night from their classrooms to their dorms. The interview is at 10:00 a.m. His physical education class ends at 9:40 a.m., giving him just enough time to make the twenty-minute walk across campus to the security office. Applying what you know about the guidelines for interviews, what advice will you give him and why?

Chapter 14: Electronically Mediated Interpersonal Communication

Interactive Chapter Outline

I.   The oral communication revolution is taking place on cellular and digital telephones.

    A.   In 2001, there were 111 million mobile-phone subscribers in the United States.

    At the present, I remain a holdout to this revolution. Are you a cellular or digital phone owner? If so, why?

    _____

    _____

    B.   Mobile phones cause many to feel safer and/or feel that they have more control of their lives.

    On a recent visit to the home of my daughter, I needed to make a quick call to a friend. After scanning my daughter's kitchen searching for the phone, it occurred to me that the only phone Kelly owned was a cellular phone, and she had taken it to work with her. I drove two miles to the nearest PDQ, stood at an outdoor phone booth in below zero weather, cursed the cellular revolution, and felt like a troglodyte. Have you used your cell phone to get help for yourself? For others? Has a cell phone helped you feel more "in control"? Explain.

    _____

    _____

    _____

II.   The Internet, an international electronic computer network, is available to many.

    A.   Internet users are familiar with Internet terminology.
        1.   World Wide Web (WWW) is a part of the Internet where information is presented in a highly visual, often multimedia, format.

        2.   A Web page presents information.

        3.   A Web site is a collection of Web pages.

        4.   A Home page is the "first" page at a Web site and shows you how to find the site.

5. A browser is a software program that enables you to look over the information on millions of Web sites. Netscape Navigator and Microsoft's Internet Explorer are two examples of browsers.

    What browser do you use most often? Why? What are some advantages and disadvantages of browsers you have used?

    _____

    _____

6. A Uniform Resource Locator (URL) is the path name of a document, more commonly known as the document's address.

7. A bookmark is a Netscape file used to store Web site addresses for sites you plan to visit again. Other browsers use names like "Favorites" or "Hotlist." What is the name of your browser's bookmark?

    _____

8. Search engines are online software programs that search the Web for you. Those search engines include Yahoo!, AltaVista, Excite, and Lycos. Which is your favorite search engine? Why would you recommend this search engine over another search engine?

    _____

    _____

B. Easy steps allow you to initiate a search.

1. Type your topic in the blank box and click Search.

2. Locate a site match and double-click on the site.

3. If you like the site, click on "Bookmark" on the menu bar and select "add bookmark" from the pull-down menu in order to store the URL. Store the site under an affectionate name that will help you recall the site.

4. When you want to return to that Web site, go to "Bookmark" and click on the name of the site.

Do you "Bookmark" favorite sites? If yes, name one. Are there certain favorite sites that you would recommend to other students in class? If yes, which ones and why?

_____

_____

_____

III.   E-mail has advantages and disadvantages over regular mail.

    A.   E-mail is faster than traditional mail with 91% of messages arriving within 5 minutes. E-mail has become the most common means of communication among my colleagues, and yet many of my colleagues swear that they never received important messages. Have any of your messages gotten lost in e-mail cyberspace? Explain.

        _____

        _____

        _____

    B.   E-mail is public, not private. Anyone with the right software can intercept your mail. Have you ever had your e-mail messages intercepted?

    C.   E-mail, although not truly free, has no per message cost. A flat fee allows you to send as many messages as you wish per month.

    D.   E-mail is used by students to communicate with professors.

        As I was typing this line in the workbook, my "you have mail" bell rang. The message was from Sarah, a student in my Public Speaking class, who wasn't present yesterday to give her assigned speech, resulting in an automatic grade drop. Here is what she wrote: "Hi, Hoeft. I was really sick yesterday and missed class. This was the first time I could make my way out of bed to get hold of you. I was wondering if there would possibly be a chance that I could make up my speech? Am I going to be docked?" What would you do if you received this e-mail the day after your student's speech was due? Have you used e-mail to communicate with your professors? Was the experience positive? Explain.

        _____

        _____

        _____

        _____

        _____

IV. Follow guidelines when using e-mail.

    A. Take advantage of delayed feedback. Never send e-mail until you reread and edit what you have written. Have you ever sent an e-mail that you regretted? Explain.

_____

_____

    B. Include the wording that you are responding to in the e-mail. The original letter writer may have long since forgotten what he/she wrote.

    C. Take into account the absence of nonverbal cues to meaning. Choose your words very carefully and add adjectives to compensate for the absence of nonverbals. I just wrote a satirical piece on the university's merit system and sent it to faculty via e-mail. One of my colleagues missed the satire and e-mailed back asking me to verify the fact I used. Oops! Has someone misunderstood one of your e-mails? Explain.

_____

_____

    D. Use common abbreviations sparingly, if at all. Take the time to write out the message and AVOID all-uppercase messages. They tend to be perceived as threatening. I'm a real "uppercase" speaker. I also overuse "!!!!" Do you have certain e-mail writing traits that may be perceived as threatening?

    E. Treat e-mail messages as you would other public communications. If you write something confidential, it could be used against you or could be misinterpreted.

    Recently, I wrote to an administrator, "Do you want me at the meeting, even if my colleague is unable to come?" He responded, "I want you." I responded, "Is it alright to say 'You want me' over e-mail?" After I pushed the send button, I realized that my "teasing reply," if viewed out of context, could get both of us into trouble. Have you or someone you know gotten into trouble as a result of an e-mail message? Explain.

_____

_____

V. The development of electronically mediated personal relationships is common.

    A. People are developing personal relationships thanks to newsgroups, Internet chat rooms, and Internet dating services.

    Several of my students and more than a few of my "middle age" friends have used Internet dating services, with mixed results. Have you developed a relationship via a newsgroup, chat room, or Internet dating service? If yes, what helpful advice would you offer a friend who is considering doing the same?

B.   Electronically mediated relationships are appealing because they present an alternative to the "bar scene." Based upon your personal experience, or that of a friend, which method sounds more appealing to you, the Internet or the bar? Explain.

VI.   Online relationships have drawbacks.

A.   EM communication is less rich than face-to-face because text messages are primarily verbal.

I am presently involved in an electronically mediated personal relationship. Although we've met on several occasions, our daily communication takes place via e-mail. Don is a wonderful writer whose words are funny and affectionate, but his messages leave me longing for face-to-face communication. Have you conducted a personal relationship via the Internet? What were the strengths of this medium? The drawbacks?

B.   EM communication, conducted via keyboard entries, is slower paced than face-to-face conversations, resulting in a reduction of spontaneity.

I just received a reply to an e-mail request that I had sent. It read as follows: "It's always something. Aaaaaaarg." I was most frustrated with his intolerant response. Four hours after I read his e-mail, he came to my office to apologize.

C. EM communicators are perceived to be less supportive. Lean messages can be perceived as having little warmth.

Go to your SENT box. Examine a "reply" that you sent to a friend who was seeking your support. Did you take the time to respond to each of his/her questions? Does your tone sound sympathetic to his/her situation? Are you guilty of being a "lean" message sender? Explain.

_____

_____

_____

D. Trust evaluations are more difficult to make. Because nonverbal channels are not available, our ability to judge trustworthiness is limited.

VII. People who use electronically mediated communication to form relationships and acquire information, should be aware of risks and abuses.

A. The abuse of anonymity is possible via EM communication.

Have you or friends used the anonymity of EM communication to say things about yourself that weren't true? Explain. Kramer and Kramarae assert that women have the most to lose from fictitious identity use. Do you agree? Are you aware of more males or females who have presented themselves as people they weren't?

_____

_____

_____

_____

B. Because of the ease with which people can be preyed upon via EM communication, some rules are suggested:
1. Limit self-disclosure if the other person fails to reciprocate. Are you familiar with someone who was preyed upon as a result of EM communication?
2. Become familiar with the means available to monitor the conversations of your children. In 2003, approximately forty-two million children between the ages of two and eighteen will use EM communication. Have your parents monitored your conversations? How did that

monitoring make you feel? Will you, as a parent, monitor your child's conversations? Explain.

_____

_____

_____

_____

3.   Be familiar with software available to block access to inappropriate and objectionable sites. Have your parents or the parents of your friends blocked access to sites? What is your reaction to this move? Will you, as a parent, block your child's access to certain sites? Explain.

_____

_____

_____

_____

C.   Technological addictions, non-chemical addictions that involve human-machine interaction, can occur causing cyber relationships to interfere with real ones.

My colleague's wife became consumed with a cyber relationship, spending every night, all night, online. One day she announced to her husband that she was leaving him to pursue a life with the "man of her dreams" whom she had found online. Within three months, her marriage and her online love affair were over. Do you know someone whose cyber relationship interfered with a face-to-face relationship? Did the online relationship survive? Explain.

_____

_____

_____

_____

VIII.   The receiver's communication skills can enhance online communication.

A.   Listen actively to what the person has said by mentally voicing what you heard.

B.   Be sensitive to the person's feelings. If the message is unclear, ask for more information

C.   Paraphrase key ideas before you respond.

D.   Be supportive when a person is sharing good news.

E.   Praise a person's accomplishments.

F.   Try to comfort a person who is hurting.

I sent an e-mail to a colleague asking five questions. She responded to three. I sent her a response asking for the answers to the other two. She answered one. Do you find yourself having similar sender-receiver communication problems?

Key Terms in Chapter 14
(Define each of the terms below.)

bookmark _____

_____

browser _____

_____

chat _____

_____

FAQ's _____

_____

home page _____

_____

Internet _____

_____

lurking _____

_____

newsgroup _____

_____

search engine _____

_____

Uniform Resource Locator _____

_____

Web page _____

_____

Web site _____

_____

World Wide Web _____

_____

Interesting Sites on the Internet

http://everythingemail.net/email_help_tips.html
> Practical tips to help alleviate e-mail confusion and to make e-mail use more productive are provided by Mary Houten-Kemp.

http://www.geocities.com/SouthBeach/Breakers/5257/Chatet.htm
> Chat etiquette, on topics that range from striking up conversations to defending yourself from solicitors of sexually-explicit materials, is explained at this site.

http://www.earthvisioncellular.com/etiquette.html
> Sponsored by Earth Vision Cellular, this site provides cellular phone etiquette.

http://www.noodletools.com/debbie/literacies/information/5locate/adviceengine.html
> This site offers tips from Debbie Abilock on choosing the best search for your purpose.

http://news.devx.com/newspolicy.asp
> This site offers rules that apply to newsgroup etiquette.

http://www.aol.com/netfind/newsgroup/glossary.html
> This site presents a glossary of newsgroup terms one should know prior to venturing into a newsgroup. It also contains a link to a site discussing newsgroup etiquette.

Exercise 14.1   Name _____

I've Got Great News

Purpose: To evaluate the communication skills of those who respond to your e-mail messages.

Instructions:
A. Choose five friends and send the same e-mail message to each person announcing Good News. (Don't make something up—make it real.)
B. Complete the questionnaire at the bottom of the page.
C. Discuss your findings with a partner.
   How did each response make you feel? Why?
   Did someone not respond? Is that typical of him/her?
   How did you react to his/her failure to respond?

E-mail Questionnaire

QUESTIONS	FRIENDS				
	#1	#2	#3	#4	#5
Did he/she respond?					
How fast was response?					
Was response sensitive to your feelings?					
Was response supportive?					

Exercise 14. 2   Name _____

What's Up?

Purpose: To evaluate your online communication skills as an e-mail sender.

Instructions:
A. Enter your "messages sent" box.
B. Retrieve your five most recent "sent" messages.
C. Respond to the questions below.
D. Use the scale below to rate your e-mail communication effectiveness.
E. With a partner, discuss your reasons for the rating.

		YES	NO
1.	Do you use precise, specific, and concrete words?	___	___
2.	Do you provide details and examples?	___	___
3.	Do you describe your feelings?	___	___
4.	Do you present ideas politely?	___	___
5.	Did you understand everything you wrote?	___	___

1	2	3	4	5	6	7	8	9	10
Unclear		Somewhat Clear				Quite Clear		Totally Clear	

Exercise 14.3   Name _____

Excuse Me, Professor, While I Answer This Call

Purpose: To better understand the role that cellular phones play in the lives of their owners.

Instructions:

A. Identify five people who own cellular phones.
B. Ask them to respond to the questionnaire below.
C. With a partner, discuss your results in an attempt to determine whether cellular phones are worth owning. Share your findings with the class.

CELLULAR PHONE SURVEY

QUESTIONS	Answer YES or NO				
	#1	#2	#3	#4	#5
1. Have you used your phone for an emergency?					
2. Do you feel safer with a cellular phone?					
3. Do you feel "cool" with a cellular phone?					
4. Do you carry your cellular phone at all times?					
5. Do you use your cellular phone in quiet zones?					
6. Do you use your cellular phone at public events?					
7. Has your cellular phone use annoyed others?					
8. Do you spend "a lot" of money per month on bills?					
9. Do you spend "a lot" of time per month on your cellular phone?					
10. Do you recommend that everyone own a cellular phone?					

Exercise 14.4   Name _____

I Met My Fiancé in a Chat Room

Purpose: To explore the quality of relationships that began in chat rooms.

Instructions:
A. Identify five students who have developed at least one close relationship in a chat room and went on to actually meet the person.
B. Ask those students to complete the following questionnaire.
C. Discuss with a partner the pros and cons of developing a close relationship with someone via chat rooms. Share your findings with the class.

CHAT ROOM SURVEY

QUESTIONS	#1	#2	#3	#4	#5
1. How much time do you spend daily in a chat room?					
2. How many "close" relationships have you developed in chat rooms?					
3. How many of those "close" relationships resulted in an opportunity to meet the individual?					
4. When you met the individual was he/she the person you expected?					
5. Do you "lie" more in chat room conversations than face-to-face?					
6. Do others "lie" to you more in chat rooms than face-to-face?					
7. Is it easier for you to develop relationships in chat rooms than face-to-face?					
8. Do you believe that the relationships you have developed in chat rooms are better than your face-to-face relationships?					
9. Would you recommend chat rooms as a way to find a life partner?					
10. Would you recommend chat rooms to someone who is shy and lonely?					

Exercise 14.5   Name _____

I'd Never "Dog Pile" When I Can "Discover"

Purpose: To become familiar with the best Internet sites available to provide students with scholarly research on interpersonal topics.

Instructions:

A. Together with students in class, brainstorm interpersonal communication topics about which you would like to learn more.

B. Vote on the one topic that all students will research via the Internet.

C. Individually, find 3 articles that offer excellent interpersonal research on the selected topic, making sure that each article contains credible source and credible authority.

D. In the space below, indicate how you accessed each article, making sure to include the following:
   1. Search Engine (online software program used to search the Web)
   2. Uniform Resource Locator (document's address)
   3. Additional information needed to access the article.

E. With students in class, identify your best article and how you accessed the article.

INTERNET ARTICLES

Title of Article #1	
Search Engine	
URL	
Additional Information	
Title of Article #2	
Search Engine	
URL	
Additional Information	
Title of Article #3	
Search Engine	
URL	
Additional Information	

Exercise 14.6   Name_____

I Need Your Advice Pronto

Purpose: To evaluate the listening and responding skills of e-mail recipients.

Instructions:

A. Compose an e-mail message that solicits the advice of a friend. Do not fabricate a situation. Instead, identify a real life problem. For example: "I just had a fight with my roommate. I really like the guy, but he's a slob. I finally had it last night. I screamed at him to pick up his mess. Now, he won't talk to me."

B. After identifying your real life problem, ask five specific questions of your friend. For example:
   1. Was I wrong to call him slob?
   2. Should I have ignored his sloppiness?
   3. Should I just wait for his anger to pass?
   4. Is there something you would do to try to make amends?
   5. Do you think I should apply for a new roommate?

C. Send your e-mail message to 5 friends.

D. Complete the following form.

E. Discuss with a partner how you felt about the quality of the responses that you received. Would you use e-mail again to address a problem? Why? Why not?

E-MAIL QUESTIONNAIRE

Write out your e-mail message:

List your five questions:

1.

2.

3.

4.

5.

	Did Respond	Did not Respond	Time to Respond	# of Questions Answered
Friend #1				
Friend #2				
Friend #3				
Friend #4				
Friend #5				

SELF EXAMINATION – CHAPTER 14

True/False   If false, explain what is wrong with the statement.

___1. E-mail is private.

_____

___2. As of 1999, approximately 60% of U.S. households had computers.

_____

___3. Lurking is acceptable behavior in a newsgroup.

_____

___4. As of 2001, there were approximately 85 million mobile phone users in America.

_____

___5. The portion of the e-mail address that appears after @ is the account name.

_____

Multiple Choice

___6. Which of the following most accurately defines a browser?
   A.   part of the Internet where information is presented in a highly visual format
   B.   software program that enables you to look over the information on millions of Web sites
   C.   path name of a document
   D.   online software program that searches the Web for you

___7. Which of the following most accurately defines a Home page?
   A.   the "first" page at a Web site
   B.   the part of the Internet where highly visual information is presented
   C.   a collection of Web pages
   D.   a file used to store Web site addresses

___8. Which of the following accurately describes a URL?
   A.   a file used to store Web site addresses
   B.   a document's address
   C.   an online software program
   D.   a collection of Web pages

___9. Approximately what percent of e-mail messages arrive within five minutes?
   A.   73%   C.   91%
   B.   82%   D.   99%

___10. What is the estimated number of people who will be connected to the Internet by 2005?
   A.   50 million
   B.   100 million
   C.   1 billion
   D.   5 billion

Complete the Thought

11.   Flaming is the term used to describe _____.

12.   Because e-mail receivers tend to perceive this technique as threatening, it is recommended that e-mail senders avoid the use of _____.

Essay Questions

13.   Verderber and Verderber outline four drawbacks to online relationships. List and explain.

14.   E-mail senders can enhance their communication by observing six suggestions. List and explain.

Interpersonal Problem Solver

Below is an e-mail that you just received from a friend. You have an exam in ten minutes and don't have time to call. You'll do that later this evening. Should you respond by e-mail? If so, based upon your understanding of communication skills that enhance online communication, what will your e-mail say?

"I tried calling you last night but your phone was busy. I really wish I could have talked to you. Things aren't going well. I need a break from school and life. Help!"

SELF EXAMINATION ANSWERS

Chapter 1
1.   T
2.   F (encoders choose)
3.   F (physical context)
4.   F (series of behaviors)
5.   F (decoders assign)
6.   A
7.   D
8.   A
9.   D
10. D
11. symbols
12. process

Chapter 2
1.   T
2.   F (they change as our roles change)
3.   F (this defines self-concept)
4.   T
5.   F (results in inflated egos)
6.   B
7.   C
8.   A
9.   C
10. D
11. Working self-concept
12. Self-concept

Chapter 3
1.   T
2.   T
3.   F (describes an impersonal relationship)
4.   F (less)
5.   F (involves observation)
6.   B
7.   C
8.   A
9.   A
10. B
11   Provisional
12. Evaluative

Chapter 4
1.   T
2.   T
3.   F (are tolerant)
4.   F (uncritical, nonevaluative)
5.   F (defines denotative)
6.   B
7.   C
8.   C
9.   B
10. D
11. unnecessary marking
12   generic

Chapter 5
1.   F (men hold longer)
2.   T
3.   T
4.   T
5.   F (listeners 70% and talkers 40%)
6.   A
7.   C
8.   C
9.   D
10. A
11   monochronic
12. proxemics

Chapter 6
1.   F (negative politeness)
2.   T
3.   T
4.   T
5.   F (relevancy maxim)
6.   A
7.   D
8.   D
9.   A
10. D
11. positive politeness
12. manner maxim

Chapter 7

1.   F (attend to nonverbal cues)
2.   T
3.   T
4.   T
5.   F (active listeners question
        at appropriate times)
6.   A
7.   D
8.   B
9.   D
10. B
11   mnemonic
12. attending

Chapter 8

1.   F (social variables such as status and
        power)
2.   F (describes a feelings paraphrase)
3.   T
4.   F (describes a tangential response)
5.   T
6.   D
7.   B
8.   C
9.   D
10. A
11. perspective taking
12. empathic responsiveness

Chapter 9

1.   F (formal cultures disclose less)
2.   T
3.   F (follow a cycle of disclosing more
        and then refraining from disclosure)
4.   T
5.   F (no labels)
6.   C
7.   C
8.   D
9.   D
10. A
11. vague referent
12. constructive criticism

Chapter 10

1.   T
2.   T
3.   F (describes a reason)
4.   F (using ethical means)
5.   F (also the peripheral route)
6.   D
7.   C
8.   A
9.   D
10. D
11. aggressive
12. assertive

Chapter 11

1.   T
2.   T
3.   F (describes accommodating)
4.   F (describes ego conflict)
5.   F (not real)
6.   B
7.   B
8.   A
9.   A
10. C
11. initiating conflict
12. unaffirming nonverbals

Chapter 12

1.   T
2.   T
3.   F (women's develop more quickly)
4.   F (set some limits)
5.   F (describes women's conversation)
6.   A
7.   D
8.   C
9.   B
10. C
11. a family
12. low self-esteem

Chapter 13

1. F (not if threat to health/well-being)
2. F (more control to interviewee)
3. F (planned ahead of time)
4. T
5. F (are not included)
6. B
7. A
8. C
9. C
10. C
11. an open question
12. framing

Chapter 14

1. F (public)
2. F (35% to 45%)
3. T
4. F (111 million)
5. F (physical location follows @)
6. B
7. A
8. B
9. C
10. C
11. a hostile or negative response to a newsgroup response
12. all-uppercase messages